INSIGHT
COSTA DEL SOL

DISCOVERY
CHANNEL

APA PUBLICATIONS
Part of the Langenscheidt Publishing Group

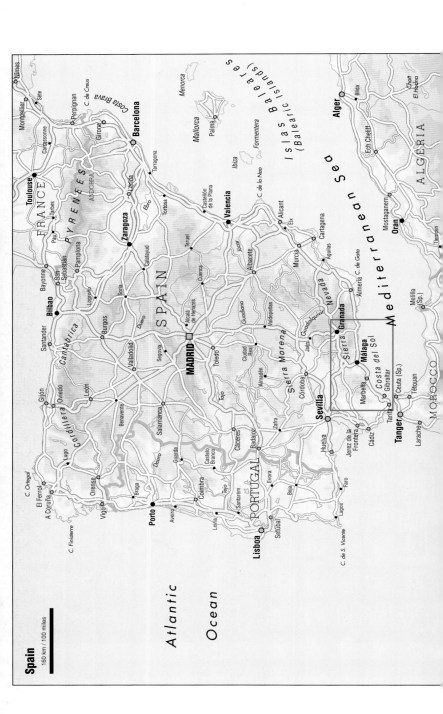

Spain

160 km / 100 miles

Welcome

This guidebook combines the interests and enthusiasms of two of the
world's best-known information providers: Insight Guides, who have
set the standard for visual travel guides since 1970, and Discovery
Channel, the world's premier source of non-fiction television programming.
Its aim is to help visitors get the most out of this beautiful region during a
short stay. With this in mind, Insight Guides' correspondent on the Costa
del Sol, Barnard Collings, has devised a range of itineraries, combining
lazy days on the beach with drives through some of Spain's loveliest scenery.

Using Marbella as a springboard (though any of the other resorts will
serve as well), he has devised 19 itineraries, ranging from walking tours of the
main resorts and short drives along the coast to longer excursions to major
attractions inland, such as the spectacularly sited town of Ronda, elegant Antequera and the famous 'white towns'. Supporting the tours are chapters
on history and culture, shopping, eating out and nightlife, plus a calendar
of events and practical information, which includes detailed hotel listings.

 Barnard Collings is a long-time resident of Marbella. He first
visited the region with friends when he was in his mid-twenties.
While his companions threw themselves into infiltrating Marbella's
high society, he set off to explore quiet inland villages. Today,
Collings is as fond as anyone of the pleasures the Costa offers,
especially its many excellent restaurants, but he retains his
passion for plunging off the beaten track to discover the
quintessential Spain.

For the 2001 edition, the late Mark Little, a regular
Insight contributor for many years,
who lived in the pretty Costa
town of Mijas, provided new
listings sections and added the
new excursions to Cádiz and
Gibraltar. The 2002 and
2004 editions were up-
dated by Josephine Quin-
tero and Sian Lézard
respectively.

LEISURE ACTIVITIES

CALENDAR OF EVENTS

PRACTICAL INFORMATION

MAPS

INDEX AND CREDITS

Pages 2/3: a taste of the good life on the Costa
Pages 8/9: a *pueble blanco* (white town) of the region

$\mathcal{C}$ *History* *& Culture*

As a travel destination, the Costa del Sol offers the best of two worlds. It is one of Europe's top leisure resorts, with modern hotels, a wide variety of gourmet restaurants, plus beaches, casinos, yacht harbours, tennis clubs and the continent's largest concentration of golf courses. Add to that a wonderfully relaxed and cosmopolitan atmosphere. On the other hand, international character notwithstanding, this is Andalucía, Spain at its most picturesque and romantic. Venture a few miles inland and you come face to face with dramatic countryside and astounding cultural treasures.

Much has changed in southern Spain, and some may lament the loss of old traditions and values in modern-day Andalucía. Others are aghast at the frenzied urban development that, in a few decades, has transformed the whole coast between Málaga and Estepona into a vast conurbation of hotels, villa developments, golf courses and marinas. But most Andalusians don't regret the disappearance from their streets of donkeys and little old ladies wearing the perpetual black of mourning. Tourism has brought prosperity and a degree of modern comfort to a land long cursed by poverty and neglect. One thing that hasn't changed is the character of the Andalusians – open and tolerant towards visitors – a character shaped by 3,000 years of history.

Cave paintings dating from 20,000–15,000BC show that Palaeolithic man flourished in southern Iberia. Skeletons, artefacts and sanctuary sites located along the coast and inland are evidence of an important prehistoric culture here. Early civilisation flourished some 4,500 years ago around Antequera, where a people about whom little is known transported enormous stone slabs, some weighing up to 180 tons, across great distances and then moved them into position to construct dolmens (cave tombs).

Greeks Bearing Gifts

The mineral wealth of the various Andalusian mountain ranges attracted sea-faring visitors. First Phoenician traders from the Middle East established settlements at Malaka (Málaga) and Cádiz in around 1000BC. Shortly afterwards Phoecean Greeks set up trading posts along the coastline. It was probably the Greeks who introduced the grape vines and olive trees that are such an essential part of the Andalusian landscape and culture today.

After the Phoenician and Greek influences waned in the Mediterranean, Carthage, the Phoenician offshoot state (in present-day Tunisia), took their place. But unlike their predecessors, who wanted only to trade with the Iberians, Carthage had territorial ambitions.

Left: the Moorish court in all its opulence
Right: figures on a Roman tomb, the Alcázar museum

The Moorish Ethic

The legacy of events that took place in southern Iberia before the unification of Christian Spain distinguishes Andalucía from the rest of the country. The most significant difference is the long Moorish presence in the region. The Moors ruled Marbella for almost 775 years before it was reconquered by the Christians some 500 years ago. Moorish Spain was a cultured Athens compared with the Spartan Christian kingdoms. In the Al-Andalus region, learning and beauty were admired, wine, women and song enjoyed. More important in Castile and the other kingdoms were the horsehair shirt and a demonstration of hard work, military prowess, statecraft and religious zeal. An Andalusian is still more likely to put off work until *mañana* if there's pleasure to be had today, and he is far more likely to admire poets than politicians or priests. The Andalusian's cavalier attitude to time, his *machismo* and indulgence of children remain prevalent today.

These were bound to conflict with the grand designs of Rome. Between 264 and 241BC, Carthage lost almost all its Iberian colonies, and by the end of the Second Punic War (219–201BC) its power base on the peninsula had been destroyed completely.

Roman construction in the area demonstrated its dominance and the physical imposition of its centralised rule over the new province. *Hispania Ulterior*, part of which was renamed *Baetica*, corresponded to today's Andalucía. Corduba (Córdoba), its administrative capital, became the peninsula's largest and richest city. Roads and aqueducts were constructed, and new cities, such as Acinipo near Ronda (whose ruins barely hint at its past glory), rose in the province. Málaga's Roman theatre exemplifies the empire's grandeur. Archaeological finds in the Marbella area hint at a Roman presence in the 1st-century BC; Marbella may have been the site of the Silniana settlement. Remnants of a bathhouse that was part of a larger complex can be seen near San Pedro de Alcántara's beach, and ruins of a Roman villa remain at the mouth of the Río Verde.

Famous Andalusian Romans

The emperors Trajan and Hadrian, the philosopher Seneca, writers Lucan and Martial, and Ossius, originator of the Nicene Creed, were among the list of illustrious Andalusian-born Romans. The Hispano-Romans spoke a language and lived by legal codes that formed the basis for those used in Spain today. In Baetica, a productive agricultural region, an indulgent ruling class

enjoyed the high life in towns and on *latifundias* (extensive estates) worked by slaves. It was a pattern that would recur throughout the region's history.

By 400, Christianity was the state religion and the Roman Empire was in decline, bringing fresh invasions from central Europe. Andalucía was occupied by the notorious Vandals; one theory holds that the name 'Andalucía' derives from the Moorish for 'land of the Vandals'. A few years later, the Germanic Visigoths, adherents of the Aryan Christianity of Byzantium, arrived on the peninsula as allies of Rome to drive out the invaders. The Visigoths encountered little opposition when in 468 they claimed Rome's Iberian provinces for themselves. The Visigoths adopted the local form of Latin and much of Roman law, and in 586 they made Catholicism their state religion. Their nobles were in constant dispute over the election of kings – in 297 years of sovereignty on the peninsula, there were 33 monarchs, few of whom died of natural causes. They never really mingled with the majority Hispano-Roman population, who tended to distrust their Germanic overlords. This distance from the natives, together with a propensity for high-level intrigues (from which the Church was not excluded), created the ideal conditions for another invasion, this time by the Muslims of North Africa, in 711.

Muslim Invasion

After an initial force landed at Gibraltar and went on to defeat the Visigoth King Roderick, an army of some 50,000 Muslims arrived. The majority were Berbers from present-day Morocco, but it was the Syrians and Arab leaders who laid the foundations for the administration, language, culture and aristocracy of their newly conquered realm, which they named Al-Andalus. Disaffected Hispano-Romans, as well as Jews, welcomed the Moors, who rapidly took control of the entire peninsula except for a handful of rebellious pockets in northern Spain and the Basque country, where Christian resistance was the greatest.

Meanwhile in Damascus, the ruling Omayyad dynasty was overthrown. Its sole survivor made his way to Al-Andalus where, in 756, he established himself as Abd al-Rahman I, with Córdoba as his capital. He began building a state in which there was considerable religious tolerance and patronage of learning and culture. In many places the Moors built on what already existed. Málaga's Alcazaba has examples of horseshoe arches – a Visigoth development – supported by Roman columns. Stones from what may have been a Roman temple were used to build the Alcazar of Marbella in the 10th century.

Abd al-Rahman III began his reign with a series of military campaigns against the Christians who were proving to be a nuisance on the northern borders. In 929, now secure in his royal tenure, he declared himself caliph, ushering in the most glorious period of Al-Andalus. In the whole Western world, Córdoba had no equal as a city, in size, splendour, culture and learning.

Left: the cultured Moors loved poetry and music
Right: a Moorish depiction of the biblical fight between David and Goliath

It would be difficult to overestimate the Moors' contribution to Andalusian culture. They introduced everything from Greek philosophy to the Arabic numbers that replaced the clumsy Roman numerals; they invented that quintessential Spanish musical instrument, the guitar; and they gave many words to the language, of which examples such as alcohol, cotton, saffron, algebra, coffee, zenith and zero later passed into English. They also introduced oranges and lemons, sugar cane and apricots, and countless herbs and spices.

Hakam II continued the enlightened and effective rule of his father but, as had been the case with the Romans and Visigoths, the upper classes lost interest in everything but their privilege and pleasure, while the masses became increasingly discontented. During most of the reign of the weak Hisham II, the militarist Almansur was the caliphate's most powerful ruler. He imposed civic discipline, initiated public works and waged successful campaigns against the Christian kingdoms, ransacking Barcelona, León and the pilgrimage city of Santiago de Compostela.

Following the death of Hisham II, the Caliphate sank into disarray. By 1031 it had splintered into 26 small kingdoms called *taifas*. This division between people is still felt in Andalucía today. Seville, the most powerful kingdom, was a stronghold of Andalusies – Muslims of Arab or Spanish descent born in Al-Andalus. Málaga, Marbella, much of the south coast and Antequera were to become part of the kingdom of Granada, a Berber bastion of the Moorish presence in Al-Andalus for another 460 years.

Christians Fight Back

Some *taifas* sought security as vassals of Christian kingdoms. These kingdoms, inspired by an increasing degree of mutual cooperation, an upsurge in religious zeal, and disunity among the Muslims, stepped up the momentum of their 'reconquest' of the peninsula. After Toledo fell to Christians in 1085, Sevilla and other *taifas* summoned the help of the Almoravids. This puritanical north African sect beat back the Christians, and then decided to stay and subjugate Al-Andalus. Their harsh rule soon proved odious to the free-thinking Spanish Moors, and terrifying for Christians and Jews. Some 60 years later the Almohads, a marginally more tolerant sect, ousted their north African rivals. They revived a failing economy, encouraged serious scholarship and constructed fine buildings, of which Seville's Giralda tower is a shining example.

The Christian victory at the battle of Las Navas de Tolosa in 1212 tolled the death knell for the Almohads and signalled the end of Muslim dominance in Al-Andalus as, one after another, their major centres fell to Christian forces. Soon only one kingdom

The 'Mudéjar' Legacy

Systems of water management still used today, and a variety of crops, fruit and herbs are among the Moors' significant legacies. Fine Moorish architecture is most grandly on show in the magnificent Mezquita of Córdoba and Granada's glorious Alhambra. In the Gothic, baroque and Renaissance buildings that were to come, it is often the addition of delicate *mudéjar* craftsmanship in wood, ceramics or stucco that is the most noteworthy feature. Moorish domestic architecture has persisted over centuries and has in modern times been adapted to meet the needs of today's urban builders: clustered villages with cube houses resemble Berber communities in north Africa; the Roman *atrium* serves as a central patio providing privacy, shade, colour and bubbling water; and, in the narrow streets, the buildings themselves act as sun shades.

remained: Granada, which also encompassed most of the province of Málaga. For nearly 250 years its Nasrid dynasty maintained independent rule by paying tribute to Christian Castile. The Nasrids were responsible for initiating the building of the Alhambra palace which, by 1390, Mohammed V had polished into the architectural marvel we see today.

The rest of Andalucía was parcelled out to Christian knights, some of whom were honoured with titles and very large *latifundia* estates. This echo of the land division of Roman times laid the groundwork for agrarian neglect and social injustice which persisted through the centuries. Many Muslims sought refuge in Granada. Those who stayed in Christian territory, the Mudejars, worked as artisans, craftsmen and agricultural labourers but, as with the Jews who served in the professions, it was hard for them to move up the social ladder without incurring the resentment of Christian citizens.

Ferdinand and Isabela

Following their marriage in 1469, Ferdinand of Aragon and Isabela of Castile ruled Christian Spain in partnership. They set out to conquer the country's last Moorish bastion and in 1485 their forces took Marbella; after a long siege, Málaga succumbed two years later; Boabdil, the last Nasrid king, surrendered Granada in 1492 and the Reconquest was complete. The subsequent persecution and banishment of Muslims and Jews, the most accomplished agriculturists and administrators, gravely damaged the region's economy.

It was in 1492 that Cristóbal Colón (aka Christopher Columbus) sailed from Andalucía and first landed in the Americas, sparking off the Spanish conquest of the New World. Much of the wealth shipped back from the 'discovery' of America was spent in an explosion of grand building. The cathedrals of Málaga and Granada are some of the great religious buildings

Above: Sala de Embajadores in the Alhambra, Granada
Right: Queen Isabela of Castile

of that time. The fortifications were strengthened in Marbella, where much of the street plan of today's Old Town was determined by the mid-16th century.

Andalucía benefited little from Spain's new, powerful status. As poor Andalusians headed for the Americas to seek their fortune, farming estates fell into neglect. Bandits preyed on travellers and the coast was vulnerable to raids by north African pirates. Most of the watchtowers along the coast date from those times. For centuries, neglect, stagnation and poverty were the rule in much of Andalucía. The whole region suffered terribly during the Spanish Civil War (1936–9) and in the subsequent 'Years of Hunger'.

Franco

Under Franco, whose dictatorship lasted for 35 years following his civil war victory, civil liberties were repressed. But the decision to allow US military bases on Spanish soil opened the door for foreign investors and visitors. Torremolinos became a fashionable resort and, along the coast, Alfonso von Hohenlohe's exclusive Marbella Club catered to the continent's rich and titled. The Costa del Sol was born.

In the 1960s, the first package tourists landed at Málaga airport. Building and catering for foreigners became the area's biggest economic activities, farms were given over to high-rise hotels, and farmers became waiters. Today the number of expats in the region is well into six figures.

Franco's death in 1975, the accession of King Juan Carlos, the reinstatement of democracy and entry into the European community ushered in a new prosperity. Prior to the quincentenary celebrations of Columbus's first voyage and its role as hosts of Expo '92, Andalucía received huge injections of investment, most noticeably – for travellers – in its motorway system.

The 'Cinderella' Resort

Marbella had a rudimentary economy based on smallholdings, fishing and iron mining when, in the early 1950s, the marquis Don Ricardo Soriano opened some chalets and a *venta* in El Fuerte. Wealthy friends and family came to stay, including his nephew, Prince Alfonso von Hohenlohe of Liechtenstein. The prince bought a fig plantation and also a *cortijo* which he transformed and opened as the Marbella Club in 1953. It set the tone for Marbella's development as a somewhat exclusive holiday resort and residential area. Other centres along the Costa del Sol opted to serve the mass market, and are now regretting it.

Above: traditional dress in a rural setting

HISTORY HIGHLIGHTS

20,000–1,000BC Prehistoric cave-dwellers populate southeastern Spain; Iberians arrive from north Africa. Mining becomes important in the Bronze Age; the fabulously rich state of Tartessos is founded near Huelva. Phoenician traders introduce the modern concepts of writing and money.

500BC Carthaginians displace the Greeks, and sack Tartessos.

201BC Rome triumphs in Second Punic War and consolidates its sovereignty throughout the Iberian peninsula.

1st century AD The Roman province of Baetica, with Córdoba as its capital, makes munificent contributions to the empire's food supply and wealth.

400 Roman Empire in rapid decline; Germanic tribes invade the peninsula. Vandals reach the south and are chased into north Africa by the Visigoths, Rome's allies.

475 Rome concedes Visigothic rule in its Iberian provinces.

711 The Visigoth King Roderick is defeated by a Muslim force from north Africa led by Tarik.

756 Abd al-Rahman I founds the Omayyad dynasty in Córdoba and becomes the first ruler of the Muslim al-Andalus.

929 Abd al-Rahman III proclaims an independent caliphate; al-Andalus reaching its zenith.

1212 The military defeat at Las Navas de Tolosa is decisive in the decline of Muslim power.

1492 Christian Spain's *annus mirabilis*: Granada, last Muslim kingdom, falls; Columbus reaches America; Jews are banished.

1600 Much of Spain's great wealth is depleted by Carlos V and Felipe II in European territorial struggles and in fighting the Reformation; culturally Spain enters its golden age. Writers Cervantes and Lope de Vega are at the peak of their powers, the Andalusian painters Velázquez and Murillo are making their names; Cano and other architects develop their baroque style.

1700 Spain's last Hapsburg king dies; Europe is plunged into the War of the Spanish Succession, from which the Bourbon Felipe V eventually emerges triumphant. The 18th century is marked by two wars with Britain.

1808–14 During the Spanish War of Independence, Napoleon's armies help themselves to Iberia's art treasures.

1900 Spain has lost all of its colonies. Reform movements in Andalucía are ruthlessly subdued.

1931 After permitting the dictator Primo de Rivera to run the country for seven years, Alfonso XIII flees the country and a republic is declared.

1936 A National Front government fails to stem political chaos. General Franco assumes the leadership of an uprising to which fellow-fascists Hitler and Mussolini lend their support.

1939 The end of a terrible three-year civil war, from which Franco emerges as the country's undisputed ruler.

1953 The US signs a defence pact with Franco; the advent of modern tourism.

1975 King Juan Carlos I begins to shepherd Spain towards democracy and into the European fold.

1982 Socialist Felipe González heads the government.

1991 The maverick independent Jesús Gil sweeps the board in Marbella's mayoral elections, ushering in a new period of regional optimism.

1992 Seville hosts Expo '92.

1999 World Athletics Championship is held in Seville's brand-new Olympic Stadium.

2002 The Euro replaces the Spanish peseta.

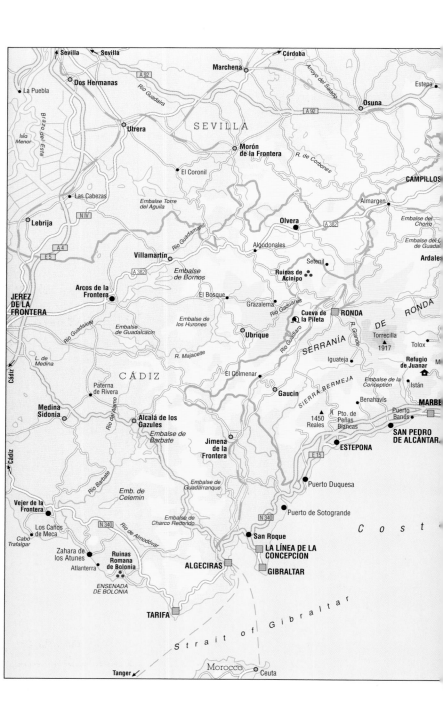

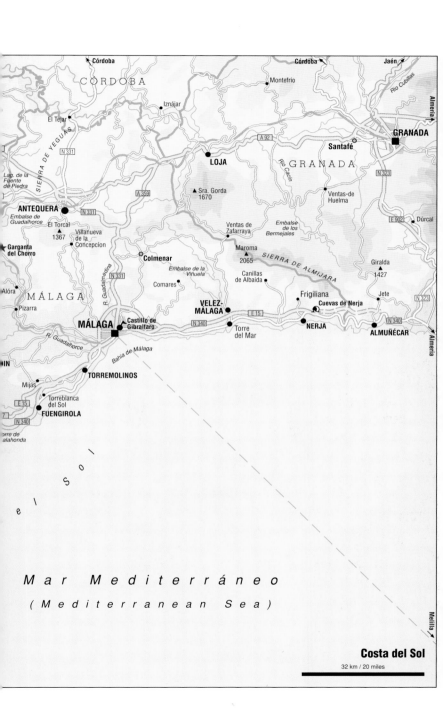

Costa del Sol

32 km / 20 miles

itineraries

Orientation

The Costa del Sol is the source of numerous clichés about Spain. As the home of sherry, flamenco and coastal resorts crammed with exuberant holidaymakers, it is a place of wine, women and song. For package tourists, it means miles of sandy beaches on the Costas – Torremolinos, Marbella and Fuengirola – and any number of nightclubs, bars, cafés, golf clubs and the 'white urbanisations' that have sprung up on what was once a rocky, unwanted coastline. Conversely, visitors attracted by the region's cultural offerings will find plenty of highlights, many attesting to the lives led by the different civilisations that have held sway here. Thus there are Roman remains, Moorish castles and Catholic cathedrals. Conservationists and those interested in ecology will also find plenty of natural wonders, from forested mountain trails and stupendous gorges and caves to lakes whose bird populations are sure to delight ornithologists.

The premise for this guide is that you will be spending about a week in the Costa del Sol area, and will be based in Marbella. The suggested itineraries, however, can easily be adapted for visitors staying in other coastal resorts. It is also assumed that, beyond the undoubted attractions of sun and sea, you will want to explore the wide range of fascinating features that can be found further afield, especially inland, with the aid of a hire car.

From Marbella to Antequera

The first four itineraries, all designed to incorporate a full day's sightseeing activities, introduce you to the historic town of Marbella and its surroundings; the port city and provincial capital of Málaga, where Pablo Picasso was born; the beautifully located town of Ronda, with its spectacular gorge; and the timeless town of Antequera. You will visit world-famous and little-known marina developments as well as traditional, isolated villages and those that have been given facelifts to meet foreign tastes. You will drive through swathes of glorious countryside that incorporate impressive natural sights and man-made creations that stand as legacies to the region's chequered history of successive in-vasions, diverse cultures and hybrid influences.

After four days of stimulation, Itinerary 5 is dedicated to an indulgent period of well-earned rest and relaxation. This is followed by nine suggested morning, afternoon and evening itineraries, all of them packed with ideas on places to see and things to do. Each itinerary contains suggestions on where to eat and drink and, where appropriate, to spend the night.

The new prosperity is bringing rapid changes to the Costa del Sol, in urban centres and *pueblos* (villages) alike. Never has there been a better time to visit.

Left: new prosperity has transformed the region
Right: inheritor of a rich and proud history

1. DISCOVERING MARBELLA *(see map, p25)*

A leisurely stroll through Marbella town; then a drive to the village of Benahavís, where you might enjoy a simple, inexpensive lunch; a look at Marbella's little sister, San Pedro de Alcántara, and a visit to the famous *pueblo* marina of Puerto Banús; an evening in Marbella's Old Town, with a fine dinner and a flamenco *tablao*.

To reach the heart of the Old Town from Marbella's central spine, Avenida Ramón y Cajal, walk up Calle Huerta Chica, then turn right to enter tiny Plaza de Victoria and exit on the right via Calle de la Estación into **Plaza de los Naranjos**, which, as its name suggests, is lined with glossy orange trees. This is the gathering place of Marbella Old Town. Before taking a table, inside or outside, at one of the bars (all are much the same and relatively over-priced), call in at the municipal tourist office, occupying a corner of the **Casa Consitorial** or *Ayuntamiento* (Town Hall) and ask if you may have the following free maps, plans and booklets: *Marbella Término Municipal Mapa y Guía*; *Marbella Casco Urbano Plano*; *Costa del Sol Occidental Guía Practica*; *Andalucía Mapa Turistico*, and the *Guía de Ocio (What's On)*, a useful monthly guide. Thus armed, you might want to peruse them over a *café con leche* in the square.

   Also on the *plaza*, the **Casa del Corregidor** (Chief Magistrate's House, built 1552) has a notable stone portico in Gothic-*mudéjar* style, an attractive

iron balcony in front of a pointed arch and a Renaissance gallery above. The fountain dates from 1504; the bust of King Juan Carlos I is somewhat younger. The plain 15th-century **Ermita de Santiago** (labelled Cofradia del S. Cristo del Amor) sits on the southwest corner.

Above: Plaza de los Naranjos
Left: a relaxing way to travel

Map in hand, wander around the Old Town for an hour. Concentrate on the maze of alleys within the perimeter of Avenida Ramón y Cajal, and *calles* Huerta Chica, Peral, Solano, Portada, Arte and Avenida Nabeul. There are plenty of shops, bars and eating places to which you may want to return. The bars range from the highly sophisticated to the characterful and trendy.

You should make a point of seeing the 17th-century **Iglesia Santa María de la Encarnación**, Marbella's main church, at which a signpost points to the **Museo del Grabado** (Mon–Fri 10am–2pm, 6–9pm; Sun 10.30am–2pm), which is devoted to exhibitions of contemporary art. Look into the tiny, 16th-century **Capilla de San Juan de Dios** and through the grille to its small ornate altar. To the northeast are remains of the **castle and town walls** (walk through Plaza de los Naranjos and up a flight of steps) first raised by the Arabs in the 9th century. Cross Avenida Nabeul into Calle Sagunto and take in the quaint and pretty pedestrianised *calles* of del Río, San Cristobal, San Ramón and Luna. (From here look out for the signposts to the **Bonsai Museum** (daily 10am–1.30pm, 4.30–8pm).

After exploring the Old Town, walk westwards along the north side of Avenida Ramón y Cajal, noticing the shops' smart window displays and the modern sculpture and fountain of *La Bella del Mar*. Cross over to the south side of the avenue into the tropical **Parque de la Alameda** and walk through its shade, past benches adorned with ceramic tiles, down the Avenida del Mar (with its collection of sculptures cast from moulds by Salvador Dalí) to reach the seafront road of Duque de Ahumada and its promenade facing Playa de Venus. Go right towards the **Puerto Deportivo** and take a leisurely walk around the port if you feel so inclined.

A Horse-drawn Carriage Ride

If you fancy a jaunt in a horse-drawn carriage, approach one of the *cocheros* and agree upon a price for a half-hour ride. You will be taken the length of the seaside promenade and into a mixed residential and commercial area bordered by Avenida Miguel Cano on the east and Calle Arturo Rubinstein on the west. During your ride you will see that development towards the west has generally been of an aesthetically pleasing design and of good quality. To the east, the old mixes with new along narrow, tree-lined streets. Make a note of any shops whose windows attract you for future reference.

For the rest of the day, exploring the nearby coast and hinterland, you will need a car. Head west on the N340, along 'the Golden Mile', passing the Marbella Club and Puente Romano hotels on the left. Remember to make a note of signs and turn-offs to other places to help establish your bearings. Puerto Banús comes up on the left with Nueva Andalucía on the right. Very soon after San Pedro de Alcántara you cross the Río Guadalmina

Above: the tiny, 16th-century Capilla de San Juan de Dios

and take a right turn to Benahavís. The Atalaya Golf and Country Club is on the left. Proceed through rural landscapes into a narrowing valley until **Benahavís** appears some 8km (5 miles) from the turn-off. Park at the village entrance and walk along its main street, Avenida de Andalucía. More than half of the 2,000 residents are foreign and Benahavís has as a result been transformed. It is now self-consciously pristine and quaint. Shops and eateries meet the needs of inhabitants and visitors from the coast alike.

The Costa del Sol's Gastronomic Corner

Benahavís, which has more than 25 restaurants, likes to think of itself as the 'gastronomic corner of the Costa del Sol'. Head to the end of Avenida de Andalucía in **La Aldea**, a stylish village-within-a-village that was the brainchild of sculptor David Marshall. His gallery here displays some of his stunning metalwork, including practical items such as candlesticks and fireguards. There are antiques and home décor shops in the small Plaza

Camilo José Cela, named after the Nobel prizewinner for literature who opened La Aldea. Take a look at the menus displayed outside the plethora of eating places and choose one for lunch. **Amanharis** (Calle del Pilar 3 tel: 952-856-026), a small hotel and restaurant has an excellent, if pricey, menu.

After lunch, drive back to the N340 and follow signs to **San Pedro de Alcántara**. The beach area here used to be delightfully undeveloped, and was popular with local families. Alas bulldozers have moved in and all is changing. At the roundabout turn into the town. Take care: the traffic whizzes past and you need considerable patience. The town does not have much to detain you except when it is celebrating a *fiesta* and a quick drive through may well be enough to satisfy your curiosity.

Nonetheless, the inhabitants and foreign residents eagerly proclaim the town's virtues and many want its independence from Marbella. If you do want to explore, park where you can, preferably along the village's main drag, Avenida Marqués del Duero, and take a walk along the avenue and through the streets to the right (east). Some of the better-quality shops can be investigated in the small mall of La Galería, *calles* Córdoba, Lope de Mena and also in the adjoining streets. End up in the Plaza de la Iglesia for some refreshment at a café alongside the church.

Back in your car, return to the N340 and proceed towards Marbella. The turn-off right into **Puerto Banús** is 3km (1¾ miles) on. Spain's first *pueblo* port, which has been the model for a number of others, opened in 1970. It is not as fashionable now as it was in its heyday, and is showing signs of wear, but it is still one of the Costa del Sol's top sightseeing attractions. See the rich collection of luxury boats and head into the backstreets to find a string of bou-

Above: Puerto Banús' *pueblo* marina.
Right: flamenco in action

tiques. Have a drink at one of the many bars – the popular **Sinatra Bar** at the far end of the front, and the **Salduba** pub next door are recommended. Head back to your hotel to rest, shower and change.

At around 9pm, head back to Plaza de los Naranjos for an aperitif. For dinner, choose one of the restaurants in the centre of Marbella. You could join the throng as you make your way towards the seafront to dine at **Restaurante Santiago** (tel: 952-770-078). This classic spot is known as one of the best places for fresh seafood in Andalucía. In summer it is pleasant to sit outside on the terrace overlooking the beach. Santiago himself, who actually hails from landlocked Castile, has a second establishment around the corner that specialises in the roast meats of his homeland. For something a bit less formal, good restaurant choices downtown include **La Pesquera** (tel: 952-778-054) on Plaza de la Victoria at the entrance to the Old Town, which is good for seafood, and **Casa Nostra** (tel: 952-861-108) on Calle Camilo José Cela 12, for Italian specialities and grilled meats; there is also a children's menu available.

If you want an Andalucían finale to your evening, head for **Flamenco Ana María** (tel: 952-775-646 or 952-860-704 Mar–Nov 11.30pm until late) on the Plaza de Santo Cristo, 4–5 blocks back in the old part of town. The flamenco show gets into full swing after midnight. Ana María's songs can give you a lump in your throat, but there are evenings when the show degenerates into a tawdry sing-along. The entrance fee includes one drink.

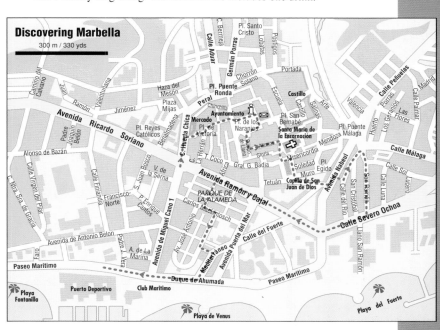

2. MALAGA *(see map below)*

Sightseeing and shopping in the provincial capital, taking in the splendid cathedral. Walk to the house where Pablo Picasso was born and tour the Moorish Alcazaba. Have lunch in Málaga or in the Parador overlooking the city, then explore the exotic botanical garden of La Concepción.

You can drive from Marbella to Málaga in one hour, or less if you take the A7 toll motorway. Try to get to the city before 10.30am.

Approaching the outskirts along the N340, follow signs to Málaga-Centro Ciudad, which will lead you into Avenida Andalucía. When you see a line of modern commercial buildings, look for the large grey **El Corte Inglés** department store ahead on the left. Bear right, around the traffic island to pass in front of the building and take the first right to its underground car park.

Walk back to Avenida Andalucía and turn left along it to cross the bridge over the Río Guadalmedina to Alameda Principal. If you are interested in modern Spanish art, you may like to visit the new **Centro de Arte Contemporaneo** (Tues–Sun 10am–2pm and 5.30–9.30pm, closed Mon; free admission), which is reached by turning right along Calle Comandante on the far side of the bridge. Calle Alemania, where the museum is located, is just off Comandante. The museum's late opening hours mean you could pay it a visit at the end of your day.

Back on the Alameda Principal, keep left and then turn left into calle Torregorda. Ahead you will see the **Puerta de Atarazanas**, an 11th-century Moorish entrance to what is now Málaga's food market. Walk through to the other end and go straight ahead until you reach the river. On your right, in Paseo de Santa Isabel is the **Museo Artes y Tradiciones Populares** (winter: Mon–Fri 10am–1.30pm, 4–7pm, Sat 10am–1.30pm; summer: Mon–Fri 10am–1.30pm, 5–8pm, Sat 10am–1.30pm). The delightful building, built

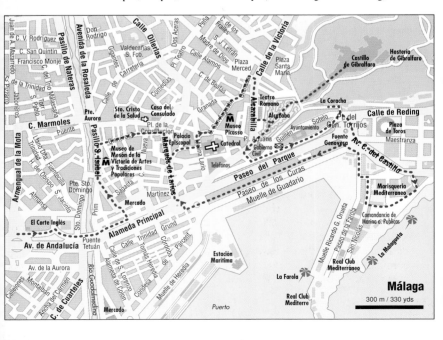

in 1632, used to be an inn run by Franciscans. In its current form as a museum of arts and popular traditions, created in 1975, it occupies three floors around a central patio.

Turn right when leaving, take the first right into Calle Cisneros and continue into Plaza de la Constitución, site of a stamp and coin market on Sundays. Notable on the north side is the **Casa del Consulado**. To the left, the **Iglesia del Santo Cristo de la Salud**, inaugurated in 1630, features typical Spanish Mannerist elements. Leave the *plaza* on the right and head into the calle Marqués de Larios, the city's main shopping street since 1886. Its construction was financed largely by the Larios family, which made its fortune from gin.

A Crippled Cathedral

Take a left turn into *calles* Strachan and Salinas and you will find yourself in front of the **Catedral** (Mon–Sat 9am–7pm; admission charge; entrance round the side), with the elaborate facade of the **Palacio Episcopal** on your left. Work on the cathedral was begun, in the Gothic style, in 1528, on the site of a former mosque. Several style changes followed and in 1782 the building evolved into what you see today. The cathedral is popularly known as *La Manquita* (The Cripple) because its other tower was never completed. The story goes that funds needed for its completion were diverted to support the American War of Independence. Inside, the most exceptional feature is the *coro* (choir), completed in 1662 by Pedro de Mena. The 40 tableaux in mahogany, cedar and red ebony are marvellously detailed. Other highlights include the Gothic Chapel of Saint Barbara, situated to the right of the central chapel of the apse. Adjoining the cathedral is the **Museo Catredralicio**, featuring religious art.

Walk along the left side of the cathedral, noting the elaborate carving on the portal and, on your left, that of the **Iglesia del Sagrario**, the surviving section of a Gothic church built in 1488. Turn left into Calle San Agustín. Midway along the cobbled street you will see the palace of the Condes de Buenavista, built in 1530–40. The austere exterior and watchtower give the building an unusual martial appearance. Inside, it is graced by a beautiful patio. The building once housed a museum of fine art, which closed to make way for a museum devoted to Málaga's most famous son, Pablo Picasso. The **Museo Picasso**, scheduled to open in 2003, has been made possible thanks to the donation of 182 of the artist's works by his daughter-in-law, Christine.

Above: *La Manquita*
Right: modern art in Málaga

At the end of calle San Agustín, turn right into the pedestrian calle Granada, which takes you to the Plaza de la Merced. On the far corner of the square is the restored **Casa Natal de Picasso** (daily 11am–2pm; also Mon–Sat 5–8pm; tel: 952-060-215), where Picasso was born in 1881. It now houses the Picasso Foundation, containing a reference library and rooms for temporary exhibitions.

Cross the square again, past the Astoria cinema, and turn right into the pedestrianised calle Alcazabilla. Cross over for a look at the **Teatro Romano**, built during the reign of Augustus and discovered by chance in the 1950s; it is being restored. Then go into the **Alcazaba** (Wed–Mon 9.30am–8pm). In the 8th century the Moors began building a fortress on the remains of a fort left by the Romans. It is connected by a rampart to the **Castillo de Gibralfaro**, a Moorish construction on Phoenician foundations,

at the top of the hill. What you see of the Alcazaba today is for the most part a construction ordered by a king of the *taifa* of Granada in 1057, which was renovated in 1933. This is an introduction to typical features of Moorish architecture: double walls with defensive towers surround gardens, patios and palaces.

Go left when leaving the Alcazaba. The solid square building on your right is the old **Aduana** (customs), constructed for the port authorities in 1829 but which now houses the central government's delegation in Málaga province. When you reach the tree-lined Paseo del Parque, continue left past the neo-baroque **Ayuntamiento** (City Hall), completed in 1919. The building's decorative features allude to the city's economic activities of the time. Tourism did not feature then and does not much now. You come to Plaza del General Torrijos and the **Fuente Genovesa**, a Renaissance fountain. One block east of the plaza is Málaga's **Plaza de Toros**, built in 1874. The area between the bullring and the seafront, called **La Malagueta**, has many good eating places and bars. Try one of the seafood houses in the area and possibly order *fritura malagueña*, a mixed fish fry that is a local speciality. Alternatively, the **Café de Paris** (Calle Velez Málaga, 8; tel: 952-225-043), not far from the lighthouse, is one of the city's best restaurants.

Elegant Gardens

Alternatively, return to the city centre, going west towards the harbour, then along the **Paseo de la Farola**, turning into the **Paseo del Parque** to walk through its elegant gardens, which have 2,000 species of flowers and trees. Many are identified with ceramic plaques. You could lunch at one of the restaurants off calle Marqués de Larios, such as the **Restaurante Chinitas** (calle Moreno Monroy 4; tel: 952-210-972) or try a selection of *tapas* from

Above: a view from Gibralfaro lighthouse

the 75-plus choice at **Bar Logueno** across the road at calle Marín García. For an extra special lunch, head back to your car and drive through Málaga and up the Gibralfaro mountain to the **Parador** (tel: 952-221-902), which stands just below the summit. Aside from good food, this hotel's restaurant offers the best views of Málaga and its bay. You might enjoy a post-prandial stroll through the recently restored Gibralfaro castle.

A Pretty Marina

A guided visit around **La Concepción Botanical Garden** (Tues–Sun 10am–dusk), on the northern outskirts of Málaga, is a pleasant way to spend the afternoon. At one time the private garden of a wealthy family, it has a large collection of exotic plants and palm trees. To get there, follow signs to Antequera until you reach the turn-off for the Jardín Histórico Botánico La Concepción. Otherwise, head back towards Marbella, following signs to Algeciras. The dual carriageway bypasses Torremolinos (save that for another visit) and the village of Benalmádena. Ignoring signs for the toll motorway, head along the coastal N 340, bypassing Fuengirola. If you have time, bear right and around to **Puerto Cabopino**. This is the newest of Marbella's *pueblo* marinas, and one of the prettiest on the coast.

A good bet for dinner in the area is one of Marbella's oldest and most famous restaurants, **La Hacienda** (tel: 952-831-267), which is located in an attractive villa in the Urbanización Hacienda Las Chapas (turn off inland from the N340 between km193 and km194). La Hacienda was the creation of the late Paul Schiff, who worked at top restaurants in Belgium for 25 years. Schiff arrived in Marbella in 1969 and his restaurant was voted a member of Relais & Chateaux in 1979. He went on to win Spain's highest gastronomic award. La Hacienda is now run by Teresa Schiff and their children. One is spoilt for choice from the selection described on the seasonal menu. Ask for advice and be inclined to choose the dishes of the day. The Gastronomic Menu (minimum two persons) consists of seven courses.

Above: the evening sun casts its spell on Alcazaba and Gibralfaro

3. RONDA *(see maps, p31 & 38)*

A scenic drive inland to Ronda, one of Spain's most spectacularly sited towns. If you want to stay the night and go horse riding in the hills the following morning (details from Ronda's tourist office), or head on to Tarifa *(see Itinerary 15, page 56)*, Ronda has lots of hotels, including the luxurious Parador (tel: 952-877-500) perched above the Tajo (gorge).

Allowing for a few stops to enjoy the views and take photographs, you can comfortably drive to Ronda from Marbella in 1½ hours.

It's a good idea to arrive by 10.30am – the light is better for photography on the outward journey before the heat haze sets in. At the eastern end of San Pedro de Alcántara, turn off the N340 onto the A376 signposted to Ronda. About 8km (5 miles) from the turn-off, a valley on the left is now **Los Arqueros Golf Course**, designed by Seve Ballesteros. Clinging to a hillside on the right are the pretty pastel-coloured buildings of La Heredia, a modern *pueblo*-style residential complex. After that you pass the luxury residential area of **El Madroñal** and **El Coto**, a hunting lodge-style restaurant specialising in meat and game.

The wide road is in good condition but its twists and turns reduce the recommended speed limit to about 50kph (30mph). Smashed crash barriers testify to the fate of drivers who have exceeded it. In early summer, vivid yellow gorse covers the lower slopes. On the left are grand views across the valley of the Río Guadalmina and undulating hills towards the coast and Gibraltar and, perhaps, Africa. You might spot eagles and vultures soaring above the region where the mountainside is at its starkest in the Serranía de Ronda, which is part of the 18,592-hectare (46,000-acre) **Parque Natural Sierra de las Nieves**. After about 35km (22 miles) you are on the high plateau of the Serranía, the road is less twisting and your average speed can rise to 80kph (50mph). Isolated hamlets lie in the basins of the *ríos* Genal and Guadiaro on the left. Shortly afterwards Ronda looms into view.

The town sits atop a rocky outcrop in a basin surrounded by the mountains of the Serranía de Ronda. It is 740m (2,428ft) above sea level, the highest of the mountains reaching some 2,000m (6,562ft). Ronda's 477 sq-km (185 sq-mile) municipal territory is one of the largest in Andalucía, yet the town and its 19 rural villages have a total of only 36,000 inhabitants. Livestock and other farming have traditionally been the main occupations.

Bandit Country

Banditry was common. The Serranía's nooks and crannies provided perfect hiding places for outlaws, who would come down from the hills to hold up a stagecoach or kidnap the son of a wealthy landowner. *Bandoleros* and tobacco smugglers were active in the area right up to the 1950s, and today

Left: the Tajo and Puente Nuevo
Right: waiting for the dance

their dubious story is told in Ronda's **Museo del Bandolero** (calle Armiñan 65; daily, winter: 10am–6pm; summer: 10am–8pm).

Stop before entering the town to look at the two gateways in the town's remaining walls. **Puerta de Almocabar**, on the right, was built in the 13th century and gave access to the Moors' *alcazaba* and town; **Puerta de Carlos V** is a typical Renaissance gateway. The wall's remnants run round to the right. Drive into the town and through the old part, to which you will return on foot. Cross the Puente Nuevo into the newer part of town, *El Mercadillo*, and try to find parking. The best bet is to go through the **Plaza de España** into calle Virgen de la Paz and take the first left to a public car park. If it's full, continue along calle Virgen de la Paz to find a space in Plaza de la Merced. Walk back to Plaza de España and pop into the tourist office for relevant information.

Across the Gorge

Ahead is the **Puente Nuevo** (New Bridge) spanning the **Tajo** (Gorge) across the Río Guadalevín and overlooked by a parador occupying the site of the old Town Hall. The bridge, built in 1751–93, reaches 98m (320ft). The architect of what has become the town's symbol died for his hat. As he was

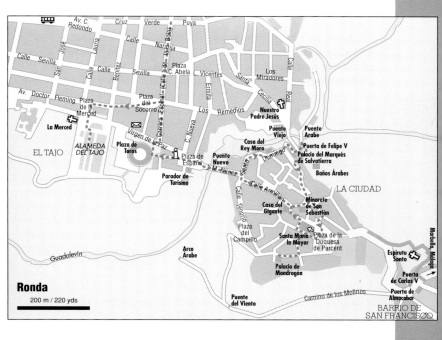

Ronda
200 m / 220 yds

being lowered in a basket to inspect his creation, the wind caught his hat. He reached out for it and fell into the gorge. The Tajo is an impressive sight that seems to hold a compelling fascination for people intent on suicide. Picadors' horses that were gored and killed by bulls used to be pushed into the gorge here.

Across the bridge, you are again in the old part of town, La Ciudad. Turn left into calle Santo Domingo. On the left, **La Casa del Rey Moro** was not the house of a Moorish king, as the name suggests, but was built in the 18th century as the town house of a wealthy family. It is now being converted into an exclusive hotel, but its attractive gardens are open to the public (daily, summer: 10am–8pm; winter: 10am–7pm; admission charge). A secret tunnel with a long, winding stairway, the Mina de Ronda, leads down to the bottom of the gorge. If under seige, the Moors used Christian slaves to carry buckets of water up the stairs. Also noteworthy are the elaborate facade, sculptured balcony and wrought-ironwork of the privately owned **Palacio del Marqués de Salvatierra**, which dates from the 18th century. The wrought iron here is typical of the work of Ronda's renowned forges: you will see much more of it around town in *rejas* (window-bar grilles) of doorways and on balconies.

Moorish Baths and Palaces

Continue left through the **Puerta de Felipe V**, a small triumphal arch built in 1742 commemorating Spain's first Bourbon king. Down the slope is the **Puente Viejo** (Old Bridge), built in 1616. From here you have an impressive upward view of the Tajo on the left. To the right is the **Puente Arabe**, definitely Moorish but perhaps originally Roman. Further right, the **Baños Arabes** public baths (Tues–Sat 9am–1.30pm, 4–6pm, Sun 10am–1pm) have the typical roof shape of Arab baths. Built in the 13th century, the baths are in a fairly good state of preservation but conservation work continues sporadically, so they are sometimes closed. Go back up to the Puerta de Felipe V and bear left up calle Marqués de Salvatierra.

As you turn right into calle Armiñán, the main street, you will see on the left the 14th-century **Minarete de San Sebastián**, which shares the Nazarene

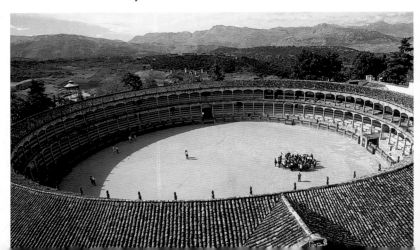

architectural style of the magnificent Alhambra palace. Next along, off to the left and up José María Holdago, is the **Casa del Gigante** (Giant's House), a Moorish palace of the same period but much changed over the centuries. Turn left here to head down the alleys to the 13th-century **St María la Mayor** mosque. A stone's throw southwest is the **Palacio de Mondragón** (Mon–Fri 10am–6pm, Sat, Sun 10am–3pm), built in 1314 by the Muslim king of Ronda. Little remains of the original save the underground passages connecting with the *alcazar* ruins.

Wander back to and across the Puente Nuevo towards the **Plaza de Toros** (daily 10am–7pm). This bullring, dating from 1785, is one of Spain's oldest. Some 200 years ago, Pedro Romero killed 6,000 bulls here. Below part of the covered terraces is a bullfighting museum. Ernest Hemingway and Orson Welles, both friends of the acclaimed Ronda matador Antonio Ordoñez; were ringside regulars. (Welles's ashes were scattered on the Ordoñez estate.) For more bullfighting memorabilia – including the edible kind, in the form of *rabo de toro* (ox tail) – go to the Restaurante Pedro Romero (tel: 952-871-110) opposite the Plaza de Toros. Other lunch options are **El Traga-buches** (calle José Aparicio 1; tel: 952-190-291), which is one of Andalucía's finest restaurants, the **Don Miguel** (calle Villanueva; tel: 952-877-722), which has good views of the Puente Nuevo, and the **Parador** restaurant (tel: 952-877-500) on the Plaza de España.

The Craft Tradition

After lunch, head up *la Bola*, as the pedestrianised Carrera Espinel is known. Here you will find plenty of shops, including tourist tat. Craft specialities – ironwork and saddlery – tend to be too bulky to carry but this is a great place to buy leather shoes and boots. Make your way back to **Plaza del Socorro** and turn left to the Plaza de la Merced and into the **Alameda del Tajo**. This park promenade was completed in 1806 with money raised from fines for indecent behaviour and blasphemy. It was certainly the scene of very indecent behaviour during the civil war when Republicans are said to have thrown 512 alleged Nationalist sympathisers from its balcony (though some claim they were hurled into the Tajo gorge).

Heading up from the park, you will soon arrive at the **Reina Victoria**. This historic hotel was built by the British in 1906 and has seen better times, but it remains the perfect spot at which to stop for refreshments on the terrace. Take a leisurely stroll through the gardens for dramatic views over the cliff. Back in your car, return across the Puente Nuevo, through *La Ciudad* and take a right turn as soon as you exit from the town. If you happen to miss this small road, stop to ask someone for the **Camino de los Molinos**. The road twists and turns through a series of olive groves and finally leads to the spot which is known to have the most impressive, most photographed views of the Tajo and Puente Nuevo. When you've finished clicking your camera, return the way you came. If you are returning to Marbella, take the C339 road.

eft: the Plaza de Toros has been the venue of bullfights since the 18th century
Above: statue of a matador – one of many exhibits at the bullfighting museum

4. ANTEQUERA *(see maps below and p48)*

See the historic architecture in the town and villages of Antequera and visit its small gem of a museum. Enter the lunar landscape of El Torcal before driving through the verdant terrain of the Montes de Málaga.

You can drive to Antequera in about 1½ hours. Take the N340 towards Málaga, then the N331. Some 40km (25 miles) from Málaga, after passing through a number of tunnels, the road reaches the highest, 780-m (2,560-ft) point of Puerto de las Pedrizas and the N331 branches off to Antequera (signposted to Seville and Córdoba). The road descends, offering the first views of Antequera's rich agricultural plain.

In land area, Antequera is the country's fifth-largest municipality, home to about 40,000 residents. Agriculture, especially cereals and olives, is the economic mainstay. Many consider the oil made from the local Hojiblanca variety of olive to be the best in Spain. Sunflowers, a new and highly productive crop here, make a vivid patchwork through the *vega* (fertile plain) in early summer. Some 12km (7 miles) further on, branch left into Antequera.

Cave Tombs

Before entering the town, look out on the right for a sign pointing to the **Conjunto Dolmenico** (Tues 3–5.30pm, Wed–Sat 10am–1pm, 4–8pm, Sun 10am–2pm). There is a car park outside the fenced-off area. Of the two dolmens here, **Cueva de Menga** is more impressive than **Cueva de Viera**. These burial chambers date from around 2500BC and little is known about the people who built them, how they managed to haul the stones, quarried in the mountains, to the site or how they raised them into position. The total weight of the 31 stones is around 1,600 tons; some of the slabs weigh 180 tons. These large cave tombs, which are 25m (82ft) deep and 3.5m (12ft)

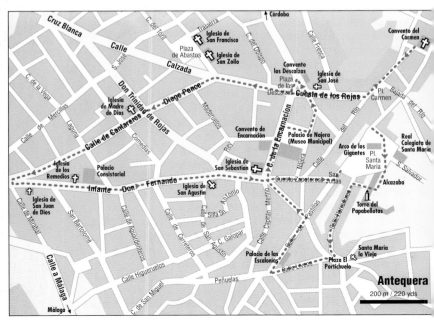

Antequera

200 m / 220 yds

itineraries

high, were then sealed and covered with earth. It is assumed they were the burial places of local leaders and their possessions, but looting over the centuries has left no evidence of either. A third dolmen, Cueva del Romeral, is 2km (1 mile) away.

A Centre of Humanism

Back in your car, drive into town and follow the signs to the Castillo or Alcazaba. Park when you reach the top of the hill. Walk through the **Arco de los Gigantes**, a Mannerist building from 1585. Looking back, it gives a picture-frame view of the town and its towers. Ahead is the facade of the **Real Colegiata de Santa María**, a huge church built in 1514–50, where, according to the plaque on its wall, a group of leading Spanish humanists taught, in defiance of theological opposition that argued that the humanistic emphasis on reason, knowledge and the centrality of man in the scheme of things was incompatible with Christian dogma. The recently restored church is now a national monument. From the side of the arch, steps lead up into what remains of the **Alcazaba**, which the Moors built in the 14th century on the remains of a Roman fortress. Now it is mostly a garden overlooked by the belltower of **Torre del Papabellotas** (Father Acorns Tower), built in 1582 with funds from the sale of a cork-oak plot. It was not long after taking the town from the Moors in 1410 that the Christians embarked on a building spree of churches and monasteries.

Look eastward and you see **La Peña de los Enamorados** (Lovers' Peak), which resembles a reclining figure. The peak is associated with a sad love story. Tazgona, daughter of a wealthy Moor from Archidona, was the secret lover of a Christian from Granada, but neither family would permit their marriage. Pursued by her father's men, they climbed the peak and jumped into the abyss to their deaths.

From the Giants' Arch, take a left down calle Herradores to the mid-18th century **Plaza El Portichuelo**, which is an ornate baroque affair. The street chapel of Santa María la Vieja, one of numerous churches repaired after the ravages of Napoleon's army, is like many seen in Mexico. In the niche of the high altar, the image of the **Virgen de Socorro** is especially revered by the townsfolk.

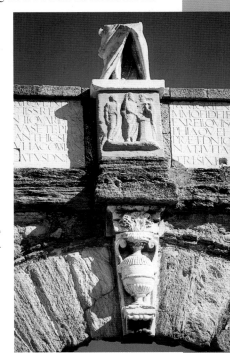

Above: Santa María la Vieja
Right: Arco de los Gigantes

Along Cuesto Alvaro de Oviedo and right into Pastillas, you will see on the right the **Casa Marques de las Escalonías**, a Mannerist-style palace from the late-16th century that exemplifies the type of town house in which local aristocrats lived. It's worth making an effort to see its Arab-style gardens, which are overlooked by three-floored galleries.

Turn left into Cuesta del Viento, descend a flight of steps, and you pass the 17th-century **Iglesia de Santo Domingo**. Dominating the *plaza* of the same name is the **Iglesia de San Sebastián**, a 16th-century Renaissance church with a striking baroque-*mudéjar* tower and an interior filled with paintings and sculpture. The *plaza*'s fountain dates from about the same time.

Down to the right of the church, and adjoining it, you will find the 16th-century Carmelite **Convento de la Encarnación**, with notable *mudéjar*

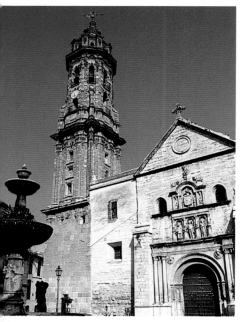

work inside. Opposite the convent is the **Palacio de Nájera**, built in the early 18th century for another rich family. Inside is an attractive patio and the **Museo Municipal** (Mon–Fri 10am–1.30pm, 4–6pm, Sat 10am–1pm, Sun 11am–1pm). This small, carefully tended museum has a singular prize: the *Efebo*, a life-size bronze figure of a garlanded boy, which was ploughed up in a field in the 1950s. Dating from the 1st-century AD and probably a copy of a Greek work, it is among the finest Roman statues found in Iberia.

Pagan Mythology

Go left down Calle Nájera, bearing left to the small, pretty Plaza de las Descalzas (Square of the Barefooted) behind which is the **Convento de las Descalzas** of the closed order of Carmelites. The convent's facade, a good example of the particular baroque style found in Antequera, somewhat ironically includes references to pagan mythology in its decoration. Turn up Cuesta de los Rojas, alongside the convent, and left past the gateway of Postigo de la Estrella to the National Monument of **Convento del Carmen**. This forms the remains of a 1633 Carmelite convent. The rich interior is dominated by three big reredos.

Return to Plaza de las Descalzas, through calle Calzada, and then right, past the market at Plaza San Francisco to the 1515 late-Gothic monument of **Iglesia de San Zoilo**. If you can, enter to see *mudéjar* plasterwork and the dome. Take calle Diego Ponce past the 18th-century **Iglesia de Madre de Dios**, a good example of Andalusian rococo architecture. When you reach the Alameda de Andalucía, turn left into calle Infante Don Fernando. On the left is a tourist office (Mon–Sat 9.30am–1.30pm, 4–7pm, Sun 10am–2pm) and the 17th-

Above: Iglesia de San Sebastián. **Top Right:** local speciality
Right: Parque Natural El Torcal

century **Iglesia de los Remedios**, dedicated to Antequera's patron saint, Nuestra Señora de los Remedios. The church's convent houses the **Palacio Consistorial** (town hall) with its 1950s neo-baroque facade and late 17th-century colonnaded cloister.

Continue along the town's principal shopping street, noting the belfry of Iglesia de San Agustín. Cross Plaza San Sebastián into Cuesta Zapateros and Cuesta San Judas, and up a hill past whitewashed houses to return to your car. For lunch you can sample fine regional dishes at **El Angelote** (tel: 952-703-465) on Plaza Coso Viejo, near the museum. Or head back to your car and follow signs to the **Parador**, whose restaurant (tel: 952-840-261) is also a good option. Stop first for *tapas* at La Espuela, a bar under the grandstand in Antequera's bullring.

Highland Maze

After lunch, take the scenic 16-km (10-mile) drive to **El Torcal de Antequera**. In these 1,200ha (2,965 acres) of protected highland you can wander among weird and wonderful limestone formations carved by the elements. There are marked paths and you are well advised to stick to them – it's easy to get lost in this maze. Ivy, wild irises, phlomis, labiates, herbs and holm oaks are among the varied vegetation. At the end of the road from El Torcal, turn right to **Villanueva de la Concepción**, a sleepy village, and head east along a pot-holed road to **Casabermeja**.

In Casabermeja follow the signpost – a camera symbol indicating a road to the right – to Málaga. This route passes through another lovely area, the **Parque Natural de Montes de Málaga**. When you rejoin the Malaga-Antequera road, follow the signs to Torremolinos or, if time allows, you may want to follow signs to the Jardín Histórico Botánico and roam the dense gardens of **La Concepción** *(see page 29)*.

5. A Day of Indulgence *(see map below)*

Recover from an extravagant lunch by spending the afternoon lazing in the sun. Alternatively try some water sports or work out in a fitness centre. Enjoy a gourmet dinner and round off the evening at a nightclub.

The plan for today resembles the itinerary followed by numerous regular visitors to Marbella for every day of their stay. This is a day devoted to total relaxation and indulgence in the Costa del Sol's great diversity of food and restaurants. The relative inactivity of this rest day should also give you the opportunity to acquire insights into the local people and their way of life.

The seafront's top hotels all have **beach clubs**. This includes two to the east of the town – Don Carlos and Los Monteros – and two on the western side – Marbella Club and Puente Romano. The features they offer are much the same, but the mix and prices vary: loungers in the sun or shade, by a pool or on the beach; changing and shower rooms with towel service; attentive waiters; barmen who know how to create a good cocktail; a buffet lunch with a wonderful array of fish, shellfish, meats, salads, fresh fruits and desserts; a variety of water sports. Opening seasons and times tend to change so telephone ahead to ensure that the beach clubs are actually open.

Water Sports Tuition

Don Carlos (N340 km192; tel: 95-276-8800), recently refurbished, has a particularly attractive, large free-style pool with islands of plants. Though the beach rates less highly, water sports facilities – windsurfing, waterskiing and sailing – are among the best on the coast and include tuition. At around €38 per head, excluding drinks, the buffet lunch is the cheapest of the four.

Los Monteros – La Cabane (N 340 km187; tel: 95-277-1700) has an outdoor pool surrounded by low thatch-roofed buildings. There is a tropical

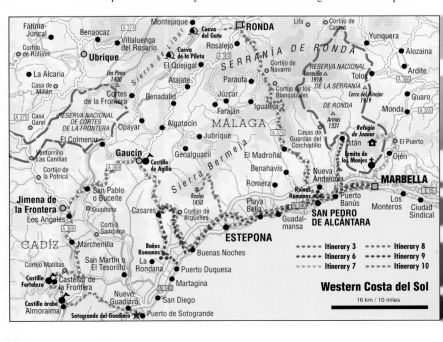

itineraries

environment within a glass enclosure that has a heated pool and terrace well screened from sea breezes. Daily live music by the pool during the summer enlivens matters, and the buffet-grill is reasonably priced. If you really want to be pampered, there is also a masseur.

The **Marbella Club** (N340 km178; tel: 95-282-2211), has the most intimate ambience. Verdant growth surrounds a freshwater pool and loungers line a beach of white sand backed by trees. A wooden jetty forms an anchorage for small craft. The fitness centre has an excellent range of equipment and an invigorating Jacuzzi; a sauna and masseur are also available. There is an excellent buffet lunch (€46), as well as an à la carte menu.

At **El Puente Romano** (N 340 km177.5; tel: 95-282-0900), a wide beach of white sand is protected by a groyne and wharf for small craft. The bar and restaurant are located in a rustic structure; the buffet is laid out in an old fishing boat in an elaborate display of the freshest fish and seafood which is prepared to order. Ask the maître d' for suggestions and explanations and check the blackboard for prices. Windsurfing gear is available for hire.

A Cheap and Cheerful Alternative

In contrast to the exclusive beach clubs is the informality of the cheap and cheerful **Victor's Beach** (N340 km177) in the urbanised Ancón area. One of the last old-style *chiringuitos* (beach bars) along the shore, it was founded in 1979 and has so far managed to resist demolition under the recent *Ley de la Costa* (Coast Law).

After devoting the afternoon to holiday pursuits such as swimming or windsurfing, or practising Andalucía's answer to yoga – the afternoon siesta – have dinner at one of the stylish restaurants along Marbella's fabled Golden Mile. You could dine at the **Marbella Club Restaurant Grill** (tel: 952-822-211). Before dinner, aperitifs are recommended in the attractive lounge bar or on the terrace. You are in the place that established Marbella's image and which is still at the heart of the town's social life.

Alternatively, across the road from the Marbella Club is **El Portalón** (tel: 952-861-075), whose menu combines classic Castillian cuisine, such as roast suckling pig, with innovative dishes

Above: last of the beach bars
Right: try your hand at water sports

made with whatever is fresh at the market. The wine bar has a fine range of Spanish wines. A third option, not far up the road past the mosque and Villa Mar y Mar, the palatial residence of King Fahd of Saudi Arabia, is **La Meridiana** (tel: 952-776-190), in Urbanización Las Lomas de Marbella. Paolo Ghirelli opened his first Marbella restaurant in 1969 and also initiated Don Leone in Puerto Banús. Since 1982 La Meridiana has expressed Ghirelli's creative flair both in the modern building's design and in the Mediterranean cuisine. Afterwards, move on a short way to the **Olivia Valère Club** (tel: 952-828-845) on the road to Istán, or head for Puerto Banús to dance away the night to live music.

6. A HALF-DAY IN ISTAN *(see map, p38)*

A leisurely morning or afternoon drive to the mountain village of Istán constitutes the perfect introduction to the lovely countryside that lies in surprisingly close proximity to the developed coastal strip.

Turn off the N340 at km177, just west of Puente Romano and the mosque. The 16-km (10-mile) long road (C427) is narrow and unmarked but should present no problem to cautious drivers. After about 2km (1¼ miles), past the Club Sierra and the last signs of urbanisation, you begin to get the impression that you are in the countryside. Big, established villas – good buys when land here was very cheap – are scattered on your left. With the Sierra Blanca rising steeply on the right, the road twists through small folding hills. Avocado and citrus trees make the valley below lush.

Soon the impressive bridge spanning the valley that carries the *autopista* toll road appears, and a bit further beyond that, the wall of the **Embalse de la Concepción**, the dam that supplies water to the coastal communities. Scrubland – some of it terraced – is dotted with juniper, gorse and wild herbs, with pockets of cork-oak and olives. Soon you are in the municipal area of **Istán**. Pine, fig, citrus and carob make an appearance, and in spring, a profusion of wild flowers. The mountain rises on the right, *cortijos* (farm estates) dot the view to the left. Just below Istán, you pass the Ermita de San Miguel in the rockface, to which the villagers make a *romería* (pilgrimage) at the end of

September. Don't be put off by the messy buildings on the approach to the village. You should find parking spaces as you enter the village.

A 9th-century Village

There is not much of note to see in Istán (population 1,300) but a stroll along the narrow, crooked *calles* gives the impression that this ancient village has changed little in domestic building style and street layout since the 9th century, when it was founded by the Moors. You can hear the

Left: Istán. **Above Right:** a traditional occupation. **Right:** *mirador* view

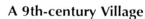

itineraries

burbling sound of running water everywhere. It's no wonder that the Moors liked the place so much. The village's sole 'monument' is the *Torre Arabe*, whose tower features a Moorish arch. It is being renovated; check at the Town Hall (tel: 95-286-9603) for visiting times.

Many locals work on the coast. Fewer now till the small plots, tend the valley's citrus trees or herd the sheep and goats that sustained the village until recently. Some run bars whose weekday regulars are retired men, with day-trippers at weekends. Have a drink and absorb some local life before returning to the Marbella road.

7. Lunch at the Refugio de Juanar *(see map, p38)*

A morning drive to the village of Ojén for lunch at a former hunting lodge in the Serranía de Ronda.

Turn off the N340 onto the A355 on the eastern edge of Marbella. It's 19km (12 miles) to the Refugio de Juanar. After you've negotiated the outskirts of Marbella the road twists up between fir and eucalyptus trees. Terraces of citrus trees are stepped down to a *barranco* (ravine) on the right. After the Venta Barranco there's a fine view of the village of **Ojén**. Take the turn-off down to the village, which faces southeast above the green valley of the Río Real where the fertile ground is cultivated to maximum effect.

Park along the main road and walk into the village. Although many of its 2,000 inhabitants now commute to work in Marbella, and much of the village has undergone modernisation, in its cobbled *calles* and *plazas* there is still the atmosphere of a typical *pueblo* – widows dressed in black contrast sharply with thick whitewashed walls, weather-beaten men sit in groups on dining chairs outside doorways, striped-curtains blowing in the breeze.

After the village the scenery becomes more dramatic as the road twists up to the 580-m (1,900-ft) high Puerto de Ojén pass. Take a turn-off to the

left (signposted to Juanar) and the road travels 5.5km (3¼ miles) into the nature reserve's stark landscape. It eventually reaches an oasis of trees surrounding the **Refugio de Juanar** (tel: 95-288-1000) where peacocks often display their plumage by way of a welcome. The Refugio was built by the state-run Parador organisation on the foundations of a Larios family *(see Itinerary 2, page 27)* hunting lodge. The staff formed a management co-operative and, with the help of the provincial authorities, they have made it a very comfortable and friendly hostelry, with an attractive pool and terraces. Game is a speciality of the kitchen, and a log fire blazes in the bar in winter (some of the bedrooms also have fireplaces). The menu of the day is excellent value at €18 and the servings could feed a giant. Alternatively, bar snacks are available.

You can walk off the effects of lunch along the 2.5-km (1½-mile) road to the **mirador**. From here, more than 1,000m (3,281ft) above sea level, there is a fine view over green valleys and hills to Marbella and, sometimes, across to Africa. If you're here at dusk, you might catch a glimpse of the wild ibex that live among the rocky crags and that often descend to drink water. Back at the *refugio*, if you're feeling energetic and have good walking shoes, you could follow part of the forested trails into the Sierra Blanca, to Istán or Ojén.

8. A MORNING IN ESTEPONA *(see map, p38)*

A morning trip to Estepona; a drive into the wooded Sierra Bermeja; a visit to Puerto de Estepona; lunch in the country or at the quayside.

It is a quick 25-km (15½-mile) journey west to the town of Estepona from Marbella. Take the coastal N340, not the toll highway. Before you reach the town you will see indications that this is becoming the next trendy area of the Costa del Sol, with fashionable new beachside property developments, golf courses and luxury hotels such as the Las Dunas and the Kempinski.

A number of new attractions might tempt you to make a detour. For horse lovers, 5km (3 miles) before the town (turn off at km159) is the **Escuela de Arte Ecuestre** (tel: 952-808-077), a riding centre that features a dressage display one evening per week – on Fridays in summer and Tuesdays in

itineraries

winter. Both adults and children will be attracted to the **Selwo Wildlife Park** (tel: 952-792-150), a 100-ha (250-acre) reserve in which lions, tigers, elephants, rhinoceros and other exotic species roam. Visitors view the resident wildlife from special buses, but to tour the park in full takes the better part of a day, so you might want to save that for a separate outing.

For now, press on into Estepona, and park along the Avenida de España, running alongside the beach. The tourist office (Mon–Fri 9am–3pm, Sat 10am–1pm) at the eastern end of the adjoining Paseo Marítimo is the place at which to ask about any special events, exhibitions and the like. Cross over into calle Santa Ana and wander at will around the old town.

An Immaculate Old Town

There is nothing of particular note but this pretty quarter is immaculately maintained – whitewashed buildings beneath tiled roofs have flower-filled balconies and solid *rejas* (grilles) across their windows. Street names are painted on ceramic tiles. In the summer cafés put out tables in the attractive **Plaza de las Flores**, once a venue for bullfights. In the Casa de Cultura at its eastern end there may be an exhibition of interest. In calle Castillo are remnants of the walls of a castle first built by Moors and rebuilt after the Christians took the town in 1456. Behind the ruins is the bustling weekday food market. The town's clock tower symbol, **Torre del Reloj**, remains from a

15th-century church. The nearby replacement parish church of Los Remedios was built in the 18th century. Wander through the back streets, keeping an eye out for art and craft shops.

There has been a great deal of residential development in Estepona in recent years. What distinguishes the municipality from others along the coast is the ongoing role of agriculture in the lives of many of its 25,000 residents. Here the development and diversification of agriculture are actively supported by the local authorities. You can see evidence of this on your drive into the Sierra Bermeja. In place of the traditional lemon-growing, more profitable tropical fruits are harvested. A monument on the Paseo Marítimo honours the honest toil of Estepona's farmers and fishermen – the town still has a big fishing fleet.

Back in your car take calle La Terraza, which dissects the old town and is signposted 'Jubrique'. The road is in a good state of repair and rises through agricultural land to the starker slopes of the Sierra Bermeja and Peñas Blancas pass. About 15km (9 miles) from the town, turn off to **Los Reales** to enter a wooded area where streams burble and roe deer, genets and foxes hide out. Marked paths lead deeper into the woods to pinsapo firs – the classical model of a Christmas tree – that are indigenous to the area and grow only at heights of more than 1,000m (3,280ft). The high point, **Alto Los Reales** (1,450m/4,757ft), looks out over the coast some 8km (5 miles) away, to Gibraltar, Africa and, on a clear day, even to Seville.

Left: Puerto de Estepona
Above: the pretty old town is immaculately maintained

Return the same way. About 2km (1¼ miles) before Estepona is the **Venta Los Reales** where you can stop for a hearty lunch of unfussy country dishes. Rabbit, cooked in various ways, is a local speciality. Travel through the town and west to **Puerto de Estepona** where the fishing fleet is anchored next to small pleasure craft and ocean-going vessels. The port does not have the glamour of Puerto Banús but is no less attractive for that. On Sunday mornings it is the scene of one of the Costa del Sol's liveliest *mercadillos* with stalls selling arts and crafts, secondhand bric-a-brac, clothes and houseware. If you did not have lunch at Los Reales, you can choose from one of the many restaurants that line the quays. Then it's back to Marbella, unless you decide to combine this trip with Itinerary 4 to Antequera *(see page 34)*.

9. A HALF-DAY IN CASARES *(see map, p38)*

A morning or afternoon drive to Casares, one of the country's most-photographed *pueblos*; a dip into the sulphurous waters where Julius Caesar is said to have bathed; lunch or dinner at a laid-back oasis among the vineyards; and, lastly, a look at the *pueblo* port of Puerto Duquesa.

Drive west along the N340 beyond Estepona, past Costa Natura (tel: 95-280-8065), Spain's first residential complex for nudists, and, just after the km147 mark turn right to Casares. There are no markings on the narrow, 14-km (9-mile) road, but it is in fair condition. As is the case when taking other such

minor roads that delve into the interior, you are soon transported into a scene that contrasts markedly with the coast's concrete ribbon. Eucalyptus trees line both sides of the road before the Sierra Bermeja's heights come into view, their rolling hills scattered with *cortijos*.

After 8km (5 miles), the road narrows and rises among corkoaks. On a bend is the rustic Venta Victoria. A little further on are good views across to the coast and, after 3km (1¾ miles), around a bend, you will find the town of **Casares**, a confection of white cubes on a mountain spur topped by the brown outline of an *alcazar*. Several roadside restaurant bars, all with pleasant terraces, overlook the town. Further on, turn left and do the locals a big favour by parking at the entrance to their *pueblo*. In Plaza de España, a typical Spanish square, is a statue of Blas Infante. Born in Casares in 1885, Infante led the Andalusian Nationalist movement, for which he was murdered by Franco's supporters. Climb the narrow, uphill *calles* to see what remains of the **Moorish castle**, or rather, as the ruins don't really amount to much, to check out an excellent vantage point. This is the site from which hundreds of *moriscos* (descendants of the Moors) who revolted against their Christian rulers in the early 16th century were hurled to their deaths.

Above: even locals stop to admire the views
Right: Gaucín village and castle

itineraries

Back on the road that skirts the town, follow signposts to Manilva and you start to appreciate a different view of Casares. Soon you see the vineyards of Manilva, which is known for both the quality of its grapes and its lively *vino de terreno*. Near a quarry on the town's edge, take a track on the left (signposted **Baños Romanos**) to the river and travel for about 1.5km (1 mile) to reach the Roman Baths. From the outside, the baths don't look much, but inside there are graceful Roman arches, and the water is invitingly clear. Julius Caesar visited these baths and locals like to believe that its waters' healing powers were responsible for curing his skin problem.

Nearby, British-run Roman Oasis (tel: 952-892-380) is a restaurant (June–Sept: evenings, and lunch on Sun) attached to a four-room hotel, the Inner Sanctum. **Manilva** is an unremarkable place but you may want to visit a back-street *bodega* (wine cellar) to sample a glass of the local *vino*. Afterwards, continue to the N340, turn right and you will reach the turn-off for **Puerto Duquesa**, another of the Costa del Sol's *pueblo* ports with the usual boutique-style shops, bars and restaurants, and an array of luxury yachts and cruisers.

10. GAUCIN, CASTELLAR AND SOTOGRANDE
(see map, p38)

Lunch in Gaucín at an old *fonda* (inn); drive into Cádiz province; visit the hideaway of Castellar de la Frontera and Sotogrande's marina.

Set out at about 11am and follow Itinerary 9 *(see page 44)* to Casares. From the road that skirts the village, turn right on the A377, signposted Gaucín. Be sure to drive carefully along the narrow 16-km (10-mile) road which, although easily navigable, can be treacherous. Falcons fly above the hushed and starkly beautiful land as the road meanders down to the Río Genal and then up the other side to **Gaucín**, which sits high above the valley.

Park whererever you can find a space in the village. One of the main sights is the 13th-century Moorish **Castillo de Aguila** (open daily 11am–1pm, 4–6pm). In 1848 the powder magazine blew up and destroyed much of the place. Gúzman el Bueno, defender of Tarifa, died here fighting the Moors in 1309. The church features a much-revered image of the Child Jesus. The

Fonda Nacional (calle Juan de Dios 8; tel: 95-215-1029) has been serving customers since the 1860s and it retains its old-world feel, although it now functions only as a restaurant. Once named the Hotel Inglés, it was frequented by the members of Gibraltar's garrison who needed an overnight stopover on the way to and from Ronda.

Bull Country

Leave Gaucín on the A369 signposted Algeciras and 2km (1¼ miles) on look back to catch a wonderful view of the village. The road drops through gorse and grass-covered hills past picturesque *cortijos* (farm estates), near which horses and cattle shelter. After 13km (8 miles) the road enters Cádiz province and crosses the Río Guadiaro. This is bull-raising country: about 3km (1¾ miles) after the hamlet of San Pablo you see a bull ranch on the left. The white profile of **Jimena de la Frontera** is outlined against a hill topped by a ruined castle. Quite a few foreigners in search of the real Spain have settled around the village, in the process affecting the 'authenticity' of what they sought.

Continue south on the A369 past meadows where cattle graze and through avenues of eucalyptus trees until, 14km (8¾ miles) from Jimena, there's a tiny road to the right leading to **Castellar de la Frontera**. The villagers abandoned this isolated place when Nuevo Castellar was built on the main road. The remains of a frontier castle that once proved to be pivotal in the struggle between Christians and Arabs broods over the newcomers' hideaway and the waters of the Embalse de Guadarranque reservoir. A narrow but very scenic road weaves southward to the A369.

Turn left and head into Nuevo Castellar, from where you can pick up a back street to Sotogrande. At the N340 coastal highway, go left (east) and then right at the sign to **Puerto de Sotogrande**. The marina's 'modern Mediterranean' style is quite different from the other *puertos* (ports) on the Costa. Here you may want to have a drink and watch the sun go down over Gibraltar. It's an easy run of 50km (31 miles) back to Marbella.

Above: the remains of a frontier castle dominate Castellar de la Frontera

11. ARDALES, LAKES AND EL CHORRO *(see map, p48)*

This itinerary, taking in Carratraca's spa, lunch in the lake district, and a visit to the spectacular El Chorro gorge, includes particularly fine scenery. If you combine this trip with Itinerary 18 *(see page 65)* you could stay overnight at the restored Hotel El Principe in Carratraca, or in a small country inn by a lake in the Ardales nature park.

Set off at around 10am and follow Itinerary 7 *(see page 41)* to Ojén. Between Ojén and Monda the road passes through a stark landscape and a small gorge. Some 19km (11¾ miles) from Marbella is the sleepy village of **Monda**, where elderly locals watch life pass by from the Central Café. The village is overlooked by a castle-like structure on a hill. This luxury hotel, the 23-room **Castillo de Monda**, was built by two Englishmen – the St George Cross occasionally flies over the ramparts. The building incorporates the remains of the original Moorish fortress, including an 8th-century tower.

Coín (pop: 18,000), described by one Moorish writer as 'a beautiful place with lots of springs, trees and fruit' is 10km (6¼ miles) on. The terracing and irrigation of the fertile surrounding area are legacies of the Moors. The locals socialise on the tree-lined *rambla* (avenue). Park nearby if you want a quick wander. The maze of narrow streets follows the old Moorish layout; new and old buildings are juxtaposed; the churches Santa María (once a mosque) and San Juan Bautista are of *mudéjar*-Renaissance style.

Museum in a Farmhouse

Leave Coín on the A355 to Cártama (take the Málaga road), passing through varied countryside. Across the Río Guadalhorce, turn left on the MA402 and head up the fertile valley where citrus and avocados grow. Near workaday Pizarra, in a converted farmhouse adjacent to an excellent restaurant, is the **Museo di Pizarra** (summer: Tues–Sun 10am–2pm, 4–8pm; winter: Tues–Sun 10am–2pm, 4–6.30pm), also known as the **Museo Hollander**, which has archaeological remains, Spanish antiques and various curiosities accumulated by the American painter Gino Hollander, who lived in these parts some years ago.

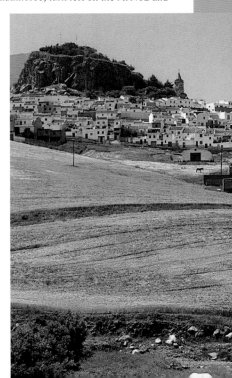

As you leave Pizarra, the outline of **Alora**'s castle appears above the white houses that drip down the hill on either side. Phoenicians, Romans, Vandals, Moors and Christians all played a role in the castle's history. Although Alora's many new buildings are evidence of the town's increased, agriculture-based prosperity, it retains much of

Right: the striking aspect of Ardales

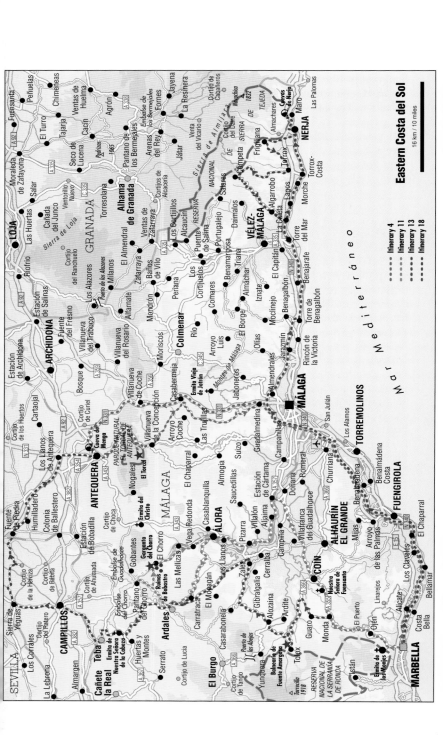

Eastern Costa del Sol

16 km / 10 miles

Itinerary 4
Itinerary 11
Itinerary 13
Itinerary 18

its old character. It took the entire 17th century to finish the construction of its enormous church, which is the second-largest in Málaga province.

From Alora head west towards Ardales, taking a scenic drive through the rugged Sierra de Alcaparain and Sierra de Aguas. Turn right for **Carratraca**, which was developed in the 19th century on the site of the '*cortijo* of foul smelling waters' to become a spa for the rich and famous. Some 600 litres (132 gallons) per minute of sulphurous waters, recommended to ease respiratory and skin complaints, gush from the ground at around 16°C (61°F). Byron and Alexandre Dumas, who made the arduous journey over the mountains to take the cures, stayed at the **Hotel El Príncipe**, which was built on the orders of Spain's King Fernando VII in the 19th century. After a period in the doldrums, the hotel was restored and reopened in 2000.

Continue through a landscape of almond and olive trees and soon **Ardales** presents a striking aspect against hills on the left. Above the white houses the ochre outlines of its castle and the *mudéjar* tower of its church stand proud. Though the Romans built the first bridge across the river below, Ardales's

roots go back much further – prehistoric paintings were discovered in local caves in 1821. To protect the cave's fragile environment, visits are limited. Call the Ardales museum (952-458-046) for information.

Bear right at the junction after the town and very soon you are in Málaga's lake district. Three reservoirs fed by the Guadalhorce and other rivers supply much of the province's water. Continue through pine trees into the **Parque de Ardales**, a recreation park. **Restaurante El Mirador**, (tel: 952-112-400) above a small tunnel, is an unpretentious place for lunch and has a good view of the reservoir. Further on, across a dam wall, is the smarter and pricier **Mesón el Oasis** (tel: 952-112-411), adjoined by the small, comfortable La Posada del Conde hotel, which opened in 2000. Note the stone seat from which Alfonso XIII opened the Guadalhorce dam scheme in 1921.

A Church Shaped from Rock

Back at the T-junction go left and a few kilometres on turn right for a drive of 6km (3¾ miles) up to the 600-m (1,968-ft) high **Ruinas de Bobastro**. In the 9th century Bobastro was Omar Al-Hafsun's fortress when he rebelled against Córdoba. Check out the *mozarabe* church shaped from the rock.

Drive downhill to **El Chorro**; on the left a wooden catwalk hangs from the cliffside. Stop when you see the entrance to the deep cleft of **La Garganta** ('The Throat'), which is popular with rock climbers. Alfonso XIII used the **Camino del Rey** ('King's Pathway) catwalk when he opened the dam, now officially closed. Continue towards Alora. On the way back to Marbella via Estación de Cártama, either go via Coín or turn left to Churriana and the N 340. You could link up with Itinerary 14 *(see page 54)*, and take in Torremolinos.

Above: an Alora farmer poses in front of his olive trees

12. FUENGIROLA AND MIJAS *(see map, p48)*

Enjoy a morning's shopping in Fuengirola followed by lunch on the promenade and an excursion to the hilltop village of Mijas.

Fuengirola is one of Spain's less hectic resorts, although it does get crowded in July and August. Its accommodation, shops, restaurants and entertainment facilities are largely addressed to young families and older people. It's a bit more expensive than Torremolinos but cheaper than Marbella, and features some 7km (4¼ miles) of continuous, well-tended and serviced beach.

If you are travelling on the coastal highway, just before crossing the river into the town of Fuengirola take a right turn to the **Castillo Sohail**. A fortification, built here by the Moors in the 10th century, was destroyed by Christians when they took the town in 1485. A new castle was built in 1730 to help control illicit trade with Gibraltar. Today it sometimes serves as a venue for exhibitions and concerts. From the castle there are good views of Fuengirola and, across the Campos de Mijas, to Mijas *pueblo* (town).

Drive into Fuengirola and follow the signposts to the **Puerto**. You will see luxury yachts berthed near traditional fishing boats against a backdrop of modern high-rises. On summer nights the Puerto area is the most animated in town. Park along the Paseo Marítimo near El Monumento del Pescador, a reminder that Fuengirola was an insignificant fishing village until a few decades ago. Walk into the fishing port and climb up onto the *mole*, a walkway that has good views of the bay, which is particularly popular in the evenings. On returning to Paseo Marítimo, turn left and then right up *calles* España or Miguel de Cervantes and dip into the pedestrian streets off them. Here you will find many of the most interesting shops, bars and restaurants. The **Plaza de la Constitución** with its underground car park is overlooked by the parish church and is a pleasant place at which to stop for a drink and to people-watch, as is the **Plaza del Ayuntamiento**, in front of the Town Hall.

The Coast's Biggest Flea Market

Fuengirola serves as a market town for much of this part of the Costa del Sol. If it is a Tuesday or a Saturday morning, follow the flow of people as they make their way towards the *Ferial* (fairgrounds) for the open-air market. On Tuesdays, the **Mercadillo** has hundreds of stalls selling cheap clothing, fruit and vegetables, souvenirs and household goods. On Saturday, there is a much more informal – and fun – atmosphere at the weekly flea market, the biggest on the coast. Try to sort the treasure from the trash as you wander around the stalls, many of which are run by British residents. Note that on certain Tuesdays and Saturdays, during *feria* (fair) time in October for example, there is no market, so call the Fuengirola tourist office (tel: 952-467-457) to check first. After exploring Fuengirola, and taking lunch at one of the restaurants on its long **Paseo Marítimo**, the seaside promenade stretching on either side of the port, head back to your car, and follow signs to **Mijas**. The road climbs 8km (5 miles) up the mountainside to this model Andalusian *pueblo* (town). Once

Left: family fun in Mijas

you arrive in the village, park in the large plaza facing the town hall. The tour coaches that choke the village every morning will probably have left by now, although the **burro taxis** that are one of the village's claims to fame might still be taking the last day trippers on a rather uncomfortable jaunt through the village streets. Foreigners outnumber Spanish residents in the extensive municipality of Mijas, which, being a typical tourist *pueblo*, is packed with brash souvenir shops. But as evening descends the town becomes quite peaceful and, wandering its back streets at leisure, you can get a pretty good impression of how it might have appeared before the tourists arrived.

The Strangest Museum

Walk through the attractive Plaza de la Constitución and past the small **Plaza de Toros** square to the main parish church, which has some mudéjar features. From the gardens beyond, you can look over the Campo de Mijas, crowded with villa complexes and golf courses, to see Fuengirola and the coast. Back near the car park is the strangest museum you are likely to encounter. The **Museo Carromato de Max** (10am–7pm, till 6pm in winter) features a varied collection of the tiniest things imaginable, such as *The Last Supper* painted on a grain of rice. A bit further on a cave serves as the shrine of the village's patroness, La Virgen de la Peña. Apparently the Virgin Mary appeared to a girl whose family lived in this cave. Votive offerings are pinned to a wall and pilgrims place flowers in front of the tiny altar. In September there's a festival in honour of the Virgin, with flamenco contests, singing and partying.

You might want to have dinner at one of the restaurants in the town, some of which have terraces overlooking the valley. Afterwards, if the spirit beckons, you can return to Fuengirola, which has a fairly active night scene. The young crowd gather at the London Pub near the seafront. But for real night-time action, head east towards the port of Benalmádena, which teems with bars and clubs, or else take in the cabaret show followed by a spot of gambling at the Torrequebrada Casino (see Itinerary 14, page 55).

Above: the aquapark at Mijas

13. La Axarquia Region, Nerja and Frigiliana
(see map, p48)

Set out at around 9am to travel east of Málaga into La Axarquía to visit the resort of Nerja and its spectacular caves.

A new dual carriageway neatly bypasses Málaga and the uninteresting beachside resort of Torre del Mar, so the drive from Marbella to Nerja should take less than two hours. This side of the coast was developed later than the environs of Marbella, and caters for Spanish and foreign families who want a quiet, cheap seaside holiday on the Costa del Sol. Fields of sugar cane, first introduced by the Moors, cover much of the flatlands. And so does plastic, under which vegetable and salad crops are grown.

Nerja has seen spectacular growth and it has not all been well controlled. Drive into the town and follow the signs to the **Balcón de Europa** – there's a car park nearby. King Alfonso XII declared this promontory to be the balcony of Europe when he visited the town in 1885 during a tour of the south coast to commiserate with the local people in the aftermath of an earthquake. The south coast lies along a geological fault line but, much like those Californians who live with a similar problem, the locals don't worry much about it. Take in the views and have some refreshments at an outdoor café.

A British Enclave
You can't help but notice the waves of variegated British accents. Nerja is very much a British enclave, and has been for many years. The town has some good shops, especially along *calles* Cristo and Pintada. Surviving among the commercialism are old houses whose heavy doorways hide plant-filled patios. Along these streets and those connecting them is an international collection of bars and eateries. Attractive beaches lie below the cliffs, small coves nearest the town, and the long Playa de Burriana to the east with the Parador (state-owned hotel) sited above it.

Some 4km (2½ miles) east on the N340, just past the aqueduct, are the **Cuevas de Nerja** (daily, summer: 10am–2pm, 4–8pm; winter: 10am–2pm, 4–6.30pm). These caves, which are among the most spectacular in the world, were discovered in 1959 by some young boys in search of bats. Since then

archaeologists have found evidence that Cro-Magnon man inhabited them some 20,000 years ago. And evidence of the Roman settlement of Detunda appears in the intensively worked patchwork of terraced plots stepping down to the sea around this delightfully unspoilt hamlet. From its *balcón* you can see the dramatic coastline of Granada province where mountains drop sharply to the Mediterranean. Return to just west of Nerja and follow the signpost to Frigiliana and the *Ruta del Sol y del Vino*.

The Fight Against Felipe II

Frigiliana appears as a white splash against the greyish lower folds of the Sierra Tejeda. Terraces of vegetables, vines and fruit trees lie below. Park at the village entrance near the old sugar factory and walk left up to the old part, where dazzling white buildings line stepped streets. Ceramic tiles tell the tale of the village's valiant fight against Felipe II's troops during the *morisco* (Moorish) rebellion of 1569. Get a translation from the **Garden Bar** (Wed–Mon; tel: 952-533-185) above the town; you might stop for lunch here if the weather is good – the barbecue and bistro menu often features succulent roast lamb, served under thatched parasols. Alternatively, for some tasty local fare, try **La Bodeguilla** (tel: 952-534-116/533-428) by the church.

A number of shops sell craft items and also Frigiliana's tasty and strong *vino del terreno*, which is typical of the Axarquía's small-scale production. The whitewashed beds you see near local *cortijos* (farm estates) are for sun-drying the moscatel grapes for raisins and wines with a high sugar content. The village is also famous for its *miel de caña* – cane molasses.

Take the road below the village and follow signs to **Torrox**. Take care on the 14km (8¾ miles) of this high, winding road. Olive trees and vines contrast with avocado and subtropical fruits. At Torrox go north to Cómpeta, 15km (9¼ miles) away through yet more attractive scenery.

Park at the **Cómpeta** entrance and visit **La Posada** (tel: 952-516-498) where potters sell their work. Village homes and *cortijos* have been modernised by foreigners here. Cómpeta is famous in the Axarquía for its *vino del terreno*. It flows freely during the *Noche del Vino* on August 15. The road zig-zags past Sayalonga and Algarrobo to rejoin the N340 some 19km (11¾ miles) away. Drive towards the setting sun.

Left: Europe's balcony. **Above:** Frigiliana
Right: life's a beach

14. TORREMOLINOS *(see map, p48)*

An evening trip to Torremolinos, the epitome of a mass-tourism resort. After dinner indulge in some flamenco or other nightlife entertainment, such as an international floor show or gambling at the casino.

Torremolinos is best explored in the early evening. Leave Marbella before 6pm and head east along the N340 motorway until you reach the exit to Torremolinos. Although the resort is as tired as it looks, local tourism authorities have carried out an urban renewal scheme to revive a town which, over the years, has provided so many good times for so many people on

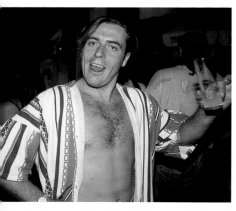

low-cost holidays. Snobbish reporters often give Torremolinos a bad press that many more open-minded visitors feel it does not really deserve. Before exploring the town centre, follow the signposts to **Playa de Carihuela** to take a stroll along a promenade lined with fish restaurants. Torremolinos's wide and well-serviced beaches are a major reason for the resort's popularity. In summer you can get a map at the tourist office on Plaza Borbollón. Back in your car, turn right at the main road and right again at the sign to calle Casablanca. Park where you can.

Crossing Casablanca is the pedestrianised **calle San Miguel**, a magnet for shoppers and strollers, which is to say, virtually everybody in Torremolinos. Calle San Miguel and the surrounding streets and arcades are packed with shops, cafés and restaurants. Prices here are generally much lower than in Marbella.

At the seaward end of San Miguel is a 14th-century Moorish *torre* (tower). Winding steeply down from the tower, the **Cuesta del Tajo** passes through what remains of the original fishing village. On the way is the 16th-century **Molino de Rosario**, one survivor of numerous flour mills that were fed by a stream, since diverted. It is from the *torre* and *molinos* that the town got its name. At the end of the walkway is Playa Bajondillo. Here and in the area of Playamar to the east you can't miss the mass of concrete high-rises lining the shore road.

Entertaining Options

Back in Calle San Miguel, take a seat at one of the numerous cafés where you can observe the passing scene and decide what you want to do for the rest of the evening and night. Here are some choices:

● You could stay in Torremolinos: have dinner and catch a flamenco show or enjoy some other form of entertainment. Off calle Casablanca, the restaurants in the Pueblo Blanco arcade give you plenty of choice. Afterwards, **Pepe Lopez** on Plaza Gamba Alegre (the other side of San Miguel) is a popular venue for flamenco.

Above: raising a glass in Torremolinos
Right: Torremolinos's Calle San Miguel, a magnet for shoppers

● There is likely to be live music at a bar nearby. If you are here in the summer, countless discos will be open, many of them concentrated around the Plaza Costa del Sol at the top of calle Danza Invisible. A young and lively disposition will stand you in good stead at any of these dance halls. **The Palladium** (Avenida Palma de Mallorca 36, a little way west of the plaza) is definitely the most spectacular nightclub in town. It has four dance floors and, should you need to cool off, a swimming pool.

● Torremolinos is very popular with gays and quite a number of places cater virtually exclusively to a gay clientele. There is a choice of scenes from suave to heavy. Particularly recommended are the La Nogalera, which crosses San Miguel and Edificio Jardín complexes.

● Instead of staying in Torremolinos, you may want to head back west along the coastal road to **Puerto de Benalmádena**, which can become seriously animated on summer nights. Here you will find an excellent choice of restaurants. For entertainment, check out the scene at one of the many music bars, or try one of the nightclubs. Younger revellers may prefer the aptly named 24-Hour Square, with its choice of discos, at the entrance of the Port.

● Another possibility is dinner, a floor show and a spot of gambling at the **Torrequebrada** hotel and casino, which you'll find around 3km (1¾ miles) from the Benalmádena harbour, heading back towards Marbella along the coastal road. Within the complex, the **Café Royal** (tel: 952-446-000) is an elegant semicircular restaurant whose wide windows give a view of the coast's glittering illuminated sweep. The menu has international staples as well as some interesting innovations. It is not cheap, but for what it offers in ambience, attentive service and clever cooking, prices are reasonable.

In the same building is the south coast's only nightclub with large-scale floor shows. The **Fortuna Night Club** stages its first show at about 10.30pm, with Spanish ballet and flamenco to the fore. At midnight there are quality international presentations. Prices are reasonable and include a drink. After the show you might adjourn to the **Casino**, which is open until 5am. Pay the entrance charge, and present your passport to gain admission.

15. TARIFA, WINDSURFING CAPITAL *(see map, p58)*

Head for the southernmost tip of the Iberian peninsula and enjoy the wide, sandy beaches of the country's windsurfing capital before seeing the Roman ruins of Baelo Claudia on Cádiz's Costa de la Luz.

Take the N340 or the toll motorway west, bypassing Estepona and Sotogrande. The unmistakable profile of the Rock of Gibraltar rises ahead as the road nears Algeciras on the Strait of Gibraltar. You will want to get through the industrial mess that surrounds Algeciras, and indeed the town itself, as fast as possible.

Once past Algeciras the road starts to round the Strait – the southernmost tip of Spain – through forests of cork-oaks, with the mountains of northern Africa visible across the water on the left. Each autumn hundreds of thousands of birds, including a multitude of vultures and eagles, congregate here as they prepare to make the crossing over the Strait to their wintering grounds in Africa. As you drive along, enormous wind-driven turbines indicate that you are approaching the wind capital of Spain.

Sacrifice of a Son

Winter winds from the southwest or northeast can reach up to 120kph (75mph). Even the average wind speed in the village of **Tarifa**, the continent's windiest spot, reaches a brisk 32kph (20mph). Incessant wind is supposed to affect a person's mental balance and one wonders how the locals hang on to their sanity. Or do they? Perhaps it was a particularly windy day in 1294 when Guzmán el Bueno ('the Good') demonstrated his determination to hold on to the town:

Above: the beach at Zahara de los Atunes
Left: Guzmán el Bueno would not surrender

he offered to sacrifice his son to the Moors rather than surrender. A Christian traitor had taken Guzmán's eldest son hostage on behalf of the Moors, who offered to hand him back if the town capitulated. Ensconced in his castle, Guzmán threw down his own dagger saying, 'Let my son be killed with an honourable weapon'. The son was indeed killed, the town relieved by Christian reinforcements and Guzmán was rewarded with large tracts of land and honours that included the founding of the aristocratic Medina Sidonia line. The current holder of the title is a left-wing duchess.

The fortifications and the solid 10th-century **Castillo de Guzmán** castle (Tues–Sun 10am–2pm, 4–6pm), which in recent years been lovingly restored, illustrate the strategic importance that the town enjoyed in former times. A world apart from the resorts east of Algeciras, Tarifa is a characterful and attractive town. A boon in water sports, especially windsurfing, has helped to enliven the narrow streets, which now feature any number of interesting shops, bars, eateries and tanned and athletic young people. Its port is also a base for scuba diving activities and dolphin-spotting excursions in summer.

Windsurfer Hangouts

If you want to absorb Tarifa's pleasant am-bience at greater leisure, you could stay at one of the town's small inns. For a more upscale choice of accommodation, there are plenty of alternatives further along the coast. These include popular windsurfer hangouts such as the aptly named Hurricane Hotel. At the long and lovely **Los Lances** beach – behind which are flourishing pine woods – there are hotels, campsites, bars, eateries, windsurf-ing schools and, for those determined enthu-siasts who throng to the most highly rated and challenging place for the sport in Europe, specialist shops.

Continue northwards along the main road, looking out for signs to the Roman ruins of **Baelo Claudia** (Tues–Sat 10am–6pm, Sun 10am–2pm) on the left. The turn-off is 15km (9¼ miles) from Tarifa, then it is an 8-km (5-mile) drive to the coastal ruins. In the heyday of the Roman empire, Baelo Claudia was a prosperous town devoted to salting fish and making *garum*, a sharp sauce from fermented fish that was all the rage in ancient Rome.

Follow the road that hugs the coast to reach the fishing village of Zahara de los Atunes, which is largely dependant on the big bluefin tuna that are netted as they make the annual migration from the Atlantic into the Strait of Gibraltar. A magnificent sandy beach stretches south beyond the luxury Atlanterra development, which is particularly popular with German tourists. Continuing along the coast you pass another tuna-fishing town, Barbate, and on through a pine forest to reach **Los Caños de Meca**.

Right: one of many squares in Tarifa that exude a pleasant, relaxed ambience

Nudists in particular enjoy the lovely pine-backed beaches here. From Los Caños you might want to make a short detour to see the **Cabo de Trafalgar** (Cape of Trafalgar), off which Britain's Admiral Nelson defeated the Franco-Spanish fleet in 1805 in a battle in which he was mortally wounded. The war between the British and the French dragged on for another 10 years, until the Duke of Wellington defeated Napoleon at Waterloo.

A Franciscan Monastery

From here, take the scenic road inland in order to reach the high-perched white town of **Vejer de la Frontera**. Although the modern world has not been allowed to make any significant inroads here, the Franciscan monastery has been converted into a small hotel and restaurant that serves tasty local dishes. From Vejer make your way back to the main N340 highway. Either turn left, to drive on to Cadíz and link up with Itinerary 17 *(see page 62)*, or head back towards the Costa del Sol. If you haven't eaten, you can dine in style at the elegant restaurant at the **Montenmedio Country Club** (tel: 956-451-216) just beyond Vejer. Alternatively, the café at the club's horse-riding centre serves more modest fare. Either way, sign up for a horse-drawn-carriage tour of the country club's huge estate.

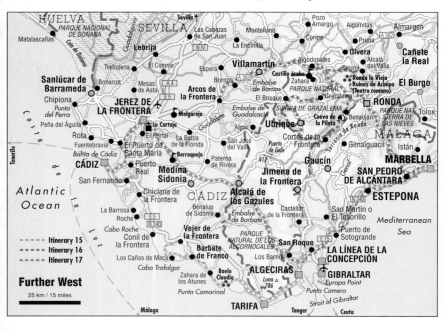

16. MOUNTAIN VILLAGES *(see map, p58)*

See Roman ruins, beautiful mountain scenery and prehistoric cave paintings, and shop for crafts. Stay overnight in Grazalema, a base for hiking in the Sierra de Grazalema, at either the Villa Turistica (tel: 956-132-162), a luxurious hotel on the outskirts of the village, or at the excellent, inexpensive Casa de las Piedras (tel: 956-132-014).

Follow Itinerary 3 *(see page 30)* to **Ronda**. After viewing the town and having lunch, take the A376 road signposted to Seville. After just a few kilometres, turn right at the sign for **Ronda la Vieja**. Following a scenic drive, look out for signs to the Roman settlement of Acinipo and its reconstructed theatre. About 8km (5 miles) on is the unusual sight of a town squeezed into a cleft. Many of **Setenil**'s houses have roofs formed by the overhanging rock, which also provides shade for the streets. One can only hope that the rock remains firmly in place. Backtrack a little way and take the road to El

Gastor through some peaceful countryside. Turn left (heading in the direction of Ronda) when you reach the A376 and after 3km (1¾ miles) turn right onto a minor road that leads to **Grazalema**.

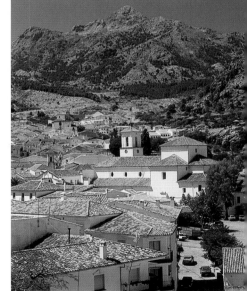

This is one of Spain's prettiest mountain villages, and its wettest. Rain-filled clouds, borne on Atlantic winds, billow up against El Torrejón and other peaks as they release their load. In some years the rainfall exceeds 3,000mm (120in). Grazalema is also a popular base for hikers. You can get information on walks in the area from the tourist office in the centre of the village.

The Villa Turistica, one of the suggested overnight stops, has great views, a swimming pool and offers self-catering accommodation. Alternatively try the comfortable Casa de las Piedras in the centre of the village – both have good restaurants. Other places to eat include El Tajo Bar Restaurant (next to the municipal pool), which has wonderful views, and the more simple Zulema bar, which offers a selection of tasty meals.

Blankets and Goat's Cheese

Wool weaving was once an important local industry – Grazalema was known for the high quality of its cloth and *mantas* (blankets) – and in the past decade various initiatives have tried to revive this skill. You can find out more at the **Fabrica de Mantas y Museo** (Mon–Thurs 8am–2pm, 3–6.30pm; tel: 956-132-008), a museum-factory to the right as you enter the village.

Left: sands near Tarifa
Right: a view from Grazalema

Opposite the camping site on the road to El Bosque you will find a factory that manufactures a product which has made the village famous far beyond the surrounding *sierras* (mountain ranges). Grazalema's *queso de cabra* is a hard goat's-milk cheese – one of the small yellow round samples makes a tasty gift. Along the 18km (11¼ miles) to **El Bosque** the road passes through a stunningly beautiful mountain landscape. Above 1,000m (3,280ft) are pinsapo firs that occur naturally nowhere else in Europe. In other parts are pines, cork-oaks, almonds, olives, carobs, poplars and eucalyptus. Past the hamlet of Benamahoma the road descends more steeply to reach a junction at which you turn right towards El Bosque. Look out for the Los Nogales municipal swimming pool on the left if it's hot and you fancy a dip.

Trout farming in fresh mountain water is a major activity in El Bosque. Its small inn, much like its counterpart in Grazalema, is called Hotel Las Truchas (tel: 956-716-061) – 'Trout Hotel'. Pick up information on hiking and horse riding from the information centre next to the municipal pool.

The road to **Ubrique** is a 16-km (10-mile) long mountainous road. Streams fill the Embalse de los Hurones on the right. Halfway into the journey, you will see the ruins of the Castillo de Tavizna rise up on the left. Many of isolated Ubrique's 18,000 population are involved in the town's thriving leather industry, which makes elegant leatherware and accessories for top labels. Rumour has it that some workshops attach pirate labels. *Piel de Ubrique* is good-quality leather from which factories or family workshops make well-designed products. You can watch work in progress and you'll probably be tempted by the goods on sale.

If it's time for lunch, find a place in town or stop at the **Venta el Chorizo** on the road to Cortes to sample its choice of sausages. The small and lonely

Above: view from the approach to Arcos de la Frontera

Cortes de la Frontera is 25km (15½ miles) away along a road that passes through more spectacular mountain scenery – the Los Pinos peak on the left rises to almost 1,400m (4,600ft). Drive through a hunting reserve that is said to be full of deer. Through Cortes head for Ronda with the Río Guadiaro on the right, and 10km (6 miles) away is the **Cueva de la Pileta** (summer 10am–1pm, 4–6pm; winter to 5pm).

The cave, discovered in 1905 by local farmer José Bullón, contains some of the most important examples of cave painting in Spain, after Altamira in Cantabria in the north. The cave walls' charcoal, yellow and red ochre paintings depict some of the things early man encountered in everyday life. If you wait by your vehicle, one of Bullón's descendants will lead you into the cave by the light of an oil lamp. Palaeolithic man left numerous traces of his habitation amid the stalagmites and stalactites carved by an underground river.

From Pileta, head north past the villages of Benaoján and Montejaque. If it is lunchtime, the **Molino del Santo** (Feb–Oct; tel: 952-167-151), a small country inn and restaurant by a river in Estación de Benaoján, is a good choice. If weather permits, dining is especially pleasant on the terrace.

Highlight of the White Towns Route

Press on to rejoin the A376, turning left for Seville. Driving westward, you will spot the village of **Zahara de la Sierra** and the ruins of its castle perched precariously on a hilltop to your left. Past the town of Algodonales, which is famous for its Spanish guitars, follow signs to **Arcos de la Frontera**, on the A382. The outline of Arcos appears stretched atop a crag rising above the lake. Follow signs to the town centre and park before entering the narrow, rising street to the Conjunto Histórico. Arcos, the highlight of the much-promoted *Pueblos Blancos* (White Towns) route, gets a lot of visitors.

To the Romans this was Arcobriga; the Moors named it Medina Arkosh and, after taking it in 1264, the Christians renamed it Arcos 'of the Frontier'. The main square, from which there are extensive views across the Río Guadalete valley, is dominated by the Plateresque facade of the Iglesia de Santa María. The church is of Visigoth origin, but was built mainly between the 16th and 18th centuries. Inside are a notable baroque choir by Roldán and paintings by Alonso Cano.

Also on the plaza, the town hall and the Arcos **Parador** hotel are in the former governor's residence, the Casa del Corregidor. You might be tempted to spend the night in this romantic, historical hotel. Nearby is the Gothic Iglesia de San Pedro with a handsome portico. Zurbarán, Pacheco and Ribera contributed to the altar paintings. From Arcos, return to the coast via Ronda, or continue on to the sherry-making town of Jerez, linking up with the next excursion.

Right: the Iglesia de Santa María

17. CADIZ AND SHERRY COUNTRY *(see map, p58)*

Taste the fine wines of Jerez and fresh shellfish at El Puerto de Santa María; visit Cádiz, the oldest city in the western world.

From Marbella, head west along the N340, past Sotogrande and San Roque, until you reach the turn-off, on the right, to **Jerez de la Frontera**. The scenic A381 takes you through the breathtaking landscape of the **Alcornocales** nature park. On either side of you spreads one of the largest cork-oak forests in the world. The bark of the trees is stripped once every nine years to be turned into corks for wine bottles. Skirting the villages of Alcalá de los Gazules and Medina Sidonia, the road takes you down into the fertile plain surrounding **Jerez de la Frontera**, the home of sherry wine.

As you enter the town, follow the signs to the **Alcázar**, and to the Bodegas Gonzalez Byass, and park in the underground car park near the Alcázar, the 12th-century castle which is the only remnant of the Moors who ruled this town for five and a half centuries until its conquest in 1264 by the Christian king Alfonso the Wise. The small fortress-palace has been carefully restored. Have a look at its miniature mosque (destined for the private use of the ruling emir) and Moorish baths. Although the Muslims were abstemious, the wine business in Jerez – initiated in Greek times in about 500 BC – continued unabated during their tenure. But it was with the arrival of British wine traders in the 18th century that the sherry business really took off. Many of the traditional sherry houses date from this period.

The grapes for sherry are grown on the chalky, white *albariza* soil of the region, then aged in large oak 'butts'. Different vintages are blended using the *criadera* and *solera* methods to ensure a consistent quality. Most of the big cellars in Jerez offer good tours of the premises, with explanations about the different types of sherry and the ageing process. One of the biggest *bodegas* (wine cellars), **Gonzalez Byass** – home of the best-selling Tío Pepe – is a large complex of cellars across the street from the Alcázar. Reserve a tour place by calling 956-357-000.

After the tour, which ends with a sherry tasting, take a look at the 18th-century **cathedral** next to the cellar, then head for Plaza del Arenal and down the pedestrian, shop-lined calle Larga street to the Alameda Cristina

and Plaza Mamelón. From here it is one block further to the **Real Escuela Andaluza de Arte Ecuestre** (Thurs at noon, also Tues in summer; tel: 956-319-635) where you can see one of the country's finest displays of horses and horsemanship shows, in which horses execute elaborate manoeuvres to music. On other days, you can visit the premises to watch rehearsals.

Shellfish Shore

Return to your car, and leave Jerez by the N-IV, heading for **Puerto de Santa María**. This town on the Bay of Cádiz was the main shipping port for sherry destined for south America and northern Europe. It also has a number of wine cellars, the best known of which is Osborne, and a castle, San Marcos, built on the site of an old Moorish mosque. But the town is most famous for its shellfish, and seafood bars line its **Ribera del Marisco** – ('shellfish shore'). Order a portion of cooked prawns, then settle in at one of the pavement tables to enjoy this delicacy with a glass of cold beer or chilled *fino* sherry.

Return to your car and follow signs to **Cádiz**. A modern bridge takes you over the Bay of Cádiz to the city, which stands on a narrow isthmus, almost completely surrounded by the sea. Turn right, and drive through the unappealing modern section of the city until you reach the entrance to the old part of Cádiz, the **Puerta de Tierra**. Its enormous stone walls are an indication of the defences needed by a port city that was a highly tempting prize for foreign invaders.

In 1587 a fleet commanded by Sir Francis Drake attacked the growing Spanish armada as it lay peacefully at anchor in the bay, before sacking the city, spreading terror up and down the coast and making off with 3,000 barrels of sherry. In less than three months during that summer, Drake's fleet captured or sank 60 Spanish fishing vessels and 40 coasters laden with materials that were intended to supply the Spanish navy. The incident was triumphantly celebrated in Elizabethan England and became known as 'the singeing of the king of Spain's beard'.

Bear left and park on the seaside promenade, Campo del Sur. Then follow the signs to the *Ayuntamiento* (town hall), on Plaza San Juan de Dios, and pick up a map at the tourist office there. The old part of the city is compact enough to be comfortably explored on foot. For your first stop, head up calle Pelota to the Plaza de la Catedral to see Cádiz's domed **cathedral**. Later, for a quick overview of the city, make your way along the narrow streets to the **Torre Tavira**. Standing at 45m (150ft), this tower is the highest point in the city,

Left: Real Escuela Andaluza de Arte Ecuestre. **Above:** a world-beating sherry
Right: the bullring at Puerto de Santa María

and is one of more than 100 that were used by the city's merchants as lookout posts for arriving ships in the days when trade with the Americas was booming. Installed in the top of the tower is a camera obscura, which projects a 360-degree view of the exterior onto a screen in a darkened room. Guides point out the main sights in the city as the image slowly revolves.

From the Torre Tavira, walk down calle Nicaragua to the chapel of Felipe Neri. This is where the first Spanish constitution was signed in 1812. Then turn right along calle San José to reach Plaza de la Mina, where the **Museo de Cádiz** is located. The museum devotes exhibition space to archaeology and to art. The most fascinating exhibits are the Phoenician sarcophagi that were discovered in this region. The Phoenicians, seafaring traders from present-day Lebanon, are said to have founded a trading post in Cádiz in 1,000BC. This suggests that Cádiz is the oldest continuously inhabited city in Europe.

Leaving Cádiz, you can return to Marbella on the narrow isthmus road that joins Cádiz to the mainland, then follow the coastal road that runs south along the Atlantic coast and round the Strait of Gibraltar, taking in the sights described in Itinerary 19 *(see page 66)*.

18. SPAS AND LAGOONS *(see map, p48)*

Take a dip in mineral-water spas (June–Oct); visit timeless villages, lakes and a flamingo sanctuary. See the stark landscapes of El Torcal and verdant views of the Montes de Málaga.

Plan on staying overnight in Antequera's Parador – phone ahead to book a room (tel: 952-840-261). Or you could splurge and stay at the sumptuous Hotel La Bobadilla (tel: 958-321-861), 30km (18¾ miles) east of Antequera. Or, if you fancy a rural retreat, try La Posada del Torcal (tel: 952-031-177), a country inn near Villanueva de la Concepción, on the southern fringes of the El Torcal nature area. Follow Itineraries 2 and 6 *(see pages 26 and 40)* as far as **Monda** and then take the MA413 and A366 via Guaro to Tolox.

Don't venture into the hillside village of Tolox but bear left up a small valley to the spa at **Balneario de Fuente Amargosa** (July–mid-Oct; tel: 952-487-462). This resort enjoys a delightful riverside setting and its waters are

Above: a gate in the stone walls that protected Cádiz from invaders
Right: Laguna de la Fuente de la Piedra, Spain's largest salt lake

itineraries

said to be good for lung and kidney ailments. Return to the A366 and, at the village of Alozaina, take the MA403, signposted to Alora. You will pass the village of Casarabonela, another white *pueblo* that clings to a mountainside, which is also famous for its mineral springs – though here the water is bottled for sale in Andalucía. Continue until you reach the hamlet of Zalea, then take the new A357 heading northwards to Ardales.

Before reaching Ardales, make a detour to Carratraca *(see Itinerary 11, page 47)*. From Ardales continue to a junction and bear left to Teba on a road that passes through fields. In Teba, located about 2km (1¼ miles) off the road and known for its leather industry, you will find shops selling reasonably priced goods. The next stop is Campillos, a lively agricultural town, also known for its leather. You can buy picnic supplies from the market next to the central church, which you can't help but notice on account of its massive Moorish doors. Then head north to sleepy Sierra de Yeguas, at which turn right towards Fuente de Piedra. (If you miss this small road, drive on to the motorway *(autovía)* and take the road to Malága for 9km (5½ miles).

The Greater Flamingo

Just before the village of Fuente de Piedra, turn right to the **Laguna de la Fuente de la Piedra** – the largest salt lake in Spain. The AMA, Andalucía's environmental agency, has a reception centre here. Between late winter and early autumn (provided there isn't a drought), the observation area offers good views of the thousands of flamingos that congregate here. This is one of only two sanctuaries in Europe where the greater flamingo still nests. The mudflats all but dry up in summer, but in spring they reach depths of around 800mm (32in) – ideal for flamingos. Other regular visitors include mallards, coots, black-headed gulls, owls, kestrels and Montague's harriers. Stilts and red-crested pochards nest here in summer; shovelers in winter.

Take the road that is signposted to **Antequera** and follow the signs to the **Parador** (tel: 952-840-261). The hotel's swimming pool will doubtless be a welcome sight if it has been a hot day, and the hotel dining room serves delicious local specialities. Tomorrow you can follow the relevant part of Itinerary 4 *(see page 34)* for sightseeing in Antequera before returning to Marbella via **El Torcal** and the **Montes de Málaga.**

19. A DAY IN GIBRALTAR *(see map below)*

Experience Gibraltar's unique mix of British and Mediterranean culture – drink draught beer at an English pub along Main Street; take a cable-car ride to see the apes, Saint Michael's Cave and the top of the Rock.

At the time of going to press, Britain and Spain were in talks regarding the future of Gibraltar. By summer 2002, Spain could have a share of sovereignty.

Drive west along the N340 and soon you will see the unmistakable profile of the British colony of Gibraltar – a 5 x 1km (3 x ½ mile) lump of limestone attached to the southern tip of the Iberian peninsula. Once you have passed Sotogrande, look for the turn-off to La Línea – Spain's border with the Rock. Leave your car in the guarded car park – there is little point in taking it into Gibraltar's narrow streets – and cross the border on foot. Don't forget to bring your passport.

Once there, you can take an Official Rock Tour, either by minibus or by taxi. The 1½-hour itinerary covers all the main sights. Or take one of the waiting buses or taxis to Market Place. Here you will see the Casemates Gate – part of the huge fortifications complex that has protected the colony through the many sieges in its history.

Moorish Namesake

Gibraltar (population: 30,000) takes its name from Jebel Tarik (Tarik's Mountain), after the Moorish chieftain whose arrival in 711 sparked the Muslim conquest of Spain. The

Above: The Rock in profile

Moors ruled the town until 1462, when it was captured by the Castilians. The Rock was taken by the British in 1704 in the Spanish War of Succession, and it became a British colony under the Treaty of Utrecht.

Cross Casemates Square to the foot of Main Street, the principal artery of Gibraltar town. On this pedestrian, shop-lined street you'll be able to appreciate Gibraltar's curious mixture of Mediterranean and British cultures. The locals slip seamlessly between English and Spanish, and taverns selling Spanish-style *tapas* stand shoulder-to-shoulder with pubs whose barmaids pull pints of English draught beer. Walk up Main Street until you reach the Anglican Cathedral, and bear right down Bomb House Lane to the **Gibraltar Museum** (Mon–Fri 10am–6pm, Sat 10am–2pm) whose exhibits relate to the history of the colony. As is the case everywhere in Gibraltar, military history predominates, but part of the building is given over to the restored 14th-century Moorish baths. Among the items on display are a copy of the first evidence of Neanderthal man ever discovered – the skull of a woman, which was found in Gibraltar in 1848.

Make your way back towards Main Street and continue south, through the Southport Gates. On the right is the small, shaded **Trafalgar Cemetery**, where British casualties of the 1805 naval battle are buried. But the remains of Admiral Nelson, who died of wounds in the battle, were preserved in a barrel of brandy and shipped back to England.

Apes' Den

Heading along Red Sands Road you come to the cable-car terminal. The cable car takes you to the Upper Rock Nature Reserve (daily 9.30am–7pm), with a stop at **Apes' Den**

halfway up. This is the place to see the renowned Gibraltar apes, the only wild monkeys in Europe. According to tradition, Britain will lose Gibraltar only when the apes leave. No less a figure than Winston Churchill ordered their preservation during World War II. A short walk from here is **St Michael's Cave**, the largest of the Rock's many caves. North of Ape's Den, along Queen's Road, are the **Upper Galleries**, or Great Siege Tunnel. The galleries were hacked out of the rock to enable Gibraltar's defenders to mount their cannons there during the siege – the 14th endured by the Rock – by French and Spanish troops in 1779–83. Return to Ape's Den and take the cable car up to the summit of the Rock for an unbeatable view, with the mountains of North Africa looming across the Strait of Gibraltar. The vista shows why Gibraltar has played such an important strategic role: here Africa meets Europe, and the Mediterranean meets the Atlantic.

The cable car takes you back to Gibraltar town. Stop at one of the Main Street bars for a pint and some typical pub grub before returning to La Línea and your car. You can link up with Itinerary 17 *(see page 62)* to explore the Cádiz coast beyond the Strait of Gibraltar.

Above: the views from Gibraltar are great, if the Barbary apes let you see them

Leisure Activities

SHOPPING

Marbella has a well-earned reputation for fancy shops with fancy prices. All of the big-name fashion houses are represented, both in the main town and, especially, in Puerto Banús. This is the place to look for high fashion, leather goods and jewellery.

For one-stop shopping that incorporates everything from food and wine to clothes, books, music, appliances, sports accessories and souvenirs, Marbella has two large complexes. The **Costa Marbella** centre near Puerto Banús is part of El Corte Inglés, Spain's largest department-store chain. The large Hipercor supermarket is located on the ground floor, while other departments are on the two upper floors. North of the town, on the Ojén road, is the **La Cañada** shopping mall, which has a large supermarket, Al Campo, and a large number of boutiques, speciality shops and fast-food outlets. This is the place to look for bargains in Marbella.

The shops in Málaga *(Itinerary 2)* are generally cheaper, and there is a wide choice of goods at the El Corte Inglés department store, and in the speciality shops and boutiques in the calle Marqués de Larios area. Torremolinos, which is especially appealing to younger tastes, and Fuengirola also offer a good and varied choice of shops *(Itineraries 12 and 14)*. And both have a less exclusive image, and generally lower prices than you'll find in Marbella. Nerja *(Itinerary 13)*, east of Málaga, is another resort town with a fair selection of quality outlets, and the choice is increasing in Estepona *(Itinerary 8)* especially for arts and crafts.

Inland, too, you should be on the lookout for interesting shops, especially if you want to buy souvenirs that represent local arts and crafts. Some of the best bargains are to be found in Ronda (antiques, boots and shoes), Grazalema (blankets), Ubrique (leather accessories), Frigiliana (ceramics, basket work) and Competa (ceramics).

Left: fans make colourful souvenirs
Right: ceramics from Frigiliana

In Gibraltar, Main Street at one time formed a shopping emporium that was especially popular with British expats on the Costa del Sol who yearned for imported goods such as tea, horseradish sauce and Colman's mustard. The colony's tax-free status made it an attractive place to buy electronic gadgets and photographic equipment. Most imported food items are now available in shops on the Costa del Sol, and the price difference for hi-fi and camera equipment is no longer that great, so the Rock has lost some of its allure as a shopper's paradise. There are still good buys, however, in cigarettes and spirits.

Marbella's Main Shopping Areas

There are shopping areas throughout the Old Town in Marbella: on Avenida Ramón y Cajal opposite the Parque de la Alameda, and at the Marbella Centre at the avenue's eastern end; along Avenida Miguel Cano and the streets west of it, including calle Alonso Bazán; on the whole stretch of Avenida Ricardo Soriano; Puerto Banús, including the nearby Cristamar and Costa Marbella complexes; Nueva Andalucía's Centro Plaza, and San Pedro's main street.

Small arcades in some of the top hotels have boutiques with a select range, mostly high-fashion clothing and accessories. There are also shops that are especially good for home-decoration items in the commercial centres that line the coastal highway.

Outdoor Markets

Mercadillos (weekly outdoor markets, 9am–2pm) are a great place for bargains. Even if you don't buy anything, a roam around the stalls gives a colourful insight into Andalusian life. *Mercadillo* prices are unbeatable. A copy of a designer cotton shirt might go for around 15 euros; a pair of blue jeans for half the price of those sold by department stores. The same goes for shoes, towels, blankets and sheets, perfumes and toiletries, and ceramics and cooking ware. And of course markets have the freshest seasonal fruit and vegetables.

The Marbella *mercadillo*, by the football ground, is open on Monday; its counterpart in San Pedro operates on Thursdays, on the calle Vega del Mar. The Nueva Andalucía art and antiques market near the bullring opens on Saturdays. The Sunday *mercadillo* in Puerto de Estepona is good for arts and crafts. The biggest outdoor market on the Málaga coast is held in Fuengirola's fairground on Tuesdays. On Saturdays the flea market at the same place has hundreds of stalls selling an incredible assortment of second-hand items.

What to Buy
Antiques

Silver and gold work, religious paintings and statues, carved and gilt picture frames, ceramic tiles, pitchers and washing bowls, handmade glass, embossed copperware, fine lace, embroidered cloth, and inlaid and rustic furniture are among the things to buy.

The big emporium at El Rastro de Río Verde (N340 km176) is a good place to find bargains. In the centre of Marbella, scout around El Arte de Giles, Edificio Marbesun and calle Jacinto Benavente. There's an outdoor antiques market on Saturday mornings near the bullring in Nueva Andalucía. Rarer finds and better buys are often found in hole-in-the-wall shops in inland villages and towns, and also in the weekly *mercadillos*,

where stallholders may not be aware of the value of something they are trying to sell.

Ronda is one of the main antiques centres in Andalucía, especially when it comes to furniture. Often though, the furniture is not genuinely antique, but rather a new creation made with old, seasoned wood. These might be fine pieces, but bear the lack of authenticity in mind when haggling over the price.

Art

Marbella's galleries don't have much art of the type worth investing in for strictly financial reasons – unless you're lucky enough to find an exhibition of works for sale by Antonio Lopez, Antoni Tàpies, Miquel Barceló or other names among the country's *firmas consagradas* ('hallowed signatures'). But southern Spain has attracted an enormous number of serious, dedicated artists, both Spanish and foreign, and there is a lot of good art to be seen on permanent exhibition and at special showings.

Recommended galleries include: Fabien Fryn's (Marbella Club, N340 km178.2), Harpe (Urbanización Torre Real, eastern exit of Marbella), El Catalejo (Urbanización Marbella Real) and Sammer Gallery, which has two branches in Puerto Banus. The serious collector will probably want to explore Málaga's galleries.

Crafts

When it comes to buying gifts and souvenirs, ceramics top the list of many visitors to the region. There are traditional utilitarian and decorative items and imaginative new shapes and designs. They are roughly or finely formed, glazed or unglazed, garishly coloured or finely painted. Some of the best known of Andalucía's ceramics, readily available from shops on the Costa del Sol, are the blue, green and white glazed ceramics from Granada, and the green ceramics from Ubeda in Jaén. Pieces range from souvenir ashtrays and vases to complete china dinner services from the renowned Cartuja de Sevilla factory. Then of course there are the unavoidable Lladró porcelain figurines from Valencia, which are much sought-after by enthusiasts throughout the world.

Ceramic shops are everywhere, and don't forget to check for bargains at the outdoor markets, where there is also plenty of choice.

shopping

Designer items for home decoration by Spain's new wave of creative talent can be found in many different media, from papier-mâché to glass and metals. These can make excellent gifts, as can goods woven from esparto or wicker. Baskets, whether for decoration or daily use, come in all shapes and sizes. Other articles include table mats, lampshades, painted wall hangings, picture and mirror frames, slippers, and all manner of decorated boxes.

There was a time when leather items were considerably cheaper in Spain than in other European countries, but this is no longer the case. Still, it is worth looking for small workshops that sell handcrafted items made to their own design. The best buys of a range of leather goods can be made directly from the leather factories in Ubrique. And don't forget to check the shoe stores on the coast for shoes and Spanish boots.

You might want to purchase some traditional fiesta dress accessories as sported by Andalusian women. These include fans, *mantillas* (lace or silk shawls worn over the head and shoulders), and decorative combs. Numerous visitors buy such items as mementos or gifts. Be warned that there is a great variation in quality. The best buys are not usually found in souvenir shops but in speciality shops used by local women.

Clothing

Clothes of comparable quality cost more in Spain (especially in Marbella) than in the United States and in other part of Europe. Children's clothing in particular is extremely expensive due to the Spanish predilection for dressing children in the finest apparel.

It is nevertheless well worth browsing the fashion boutiques of Marbella. Here you will find shops with international names such as Gucci and Benetton, but for fashionable threads, jewellery and other accessories it is perhaps best to go for the labels from the big crop of talented Spanish designers who have risen to prominence in the past decade. These include Adolfo Dominguez, Jesús del Pozo, Manuel Piña, Sybilla, Purificación Garcia, Roser Mercé, José Tomas, Toni Miró, Pedro Moreno and Vitorio y Luchino. Check out the outlets of the Spanish chain Zara for good fashion at reasonable prices.

Music

You may want to buy a classical Spanish guitar or a small flamenco model. A custom-made *guitarra española* costs a fortune; cheaper factory-made guitars produce a fine enough sound. A pair of castanets also make a fine memento. A recommended outlet for musical instruments in Marbella is La Música on Avenida Severo Ochoa 47.

There's a good selection of Spanish sounds at the Disco 2000 shop on Avenida Ramón y Cajal in central Marbella, and also at the Costa Marbella shopping centre. Here you'll find flamenco, Spanish pop and *zarzuela* – as Spanish light opera is known.

Food and Wine

The Hipercor supermarket in the Costa Marbella shopping centre near Puerto Banús is the best place for gifts and mementos of the edible kind. You might not manage a whole cured *jamón serrano* ham, but there are many more portable typically Spanish packaged foods. These include a variety of olives, capers, sherry vinegar, saffron, paprika, sausages, raisins and dried figs.

Spanish wine – the range of sherries, sweet wine from Málaga, aged reds from Rioja and Ribera del Duero, whites from Rueda and Rias Baixas, and sparkling *cava* are all great value. Spanish brandy is also a good buy. Casa Pablo in central Marbella (Gomez de la Serna 2) is a good place to look. The Hipercor supermarket also has a big selection; its house brands (sold under the name of the vineyard's region) are good value. Check out your country's customs regulations before packing the booze.

Above: Marbella has plenty of exclusive shops, where exclusive means expensive

EATING OUT

Fine food in relaxing surroundings is one of the great pleasures of visiting the Costa del Sol. Until recently, Andalucía did not have much of a restaurant tradition but, thanks to its long tradition of tourism, the southern coast has always been an exception. Marbella in particular has a wide choice of restaurants, from cheap and cheerful beach-side establishments to stylish restaurants that serve wonderfully prepared and presented cuisine. Aside from Spain's new generation of chefs, a number of chefs have come from elsewhere in Europe to ply their trade, thereby adding to the gastronomic variety. Cooks in Andalucía have at their disposal fine raw ingredients, whether it's fresh fruit and vegetables, fish and shellfish, or pork and lamb. The quality of the beef, which used to be poor, has improved considerably.

What to Order

Traditional Andalusian cuisine tends to present its ingredients as simply as possible. *Gazpacho* is a tasty liquid blend of tomatoes, peppers, garlic, oil, vinegar and (possibly stale) bread served up as a refreshing cold soup. A Málaga variation is *ajo blanco*, a cold soup made with fresh almonds and garlic and garnished with grapes.

Seafood is a recurring ingredient in many soups and in stews such as *zarzuela de mariscos*, but is usually eaten either plainly grilled or *a la sal* – baked in a crust of salt.

The local speciality is fried fish – anchovies, squid, hake, baby sole – whose quality depends on the freshness of the fish and the standard of the oil. Ask for *fritura Malagueña* if you want to try a platter of assorted fried fish.

Renewed interest in Andalusia's Moorish history has seen the triumphant return of such recipes as lamb roasted with honey. Regional specialities from elsewhere in Spain, particularly the Basque country, are also represented on Costa del Sol menus.

Paella, the national dish, originated in Valencia. Saffron-flavoured rice is garnished with diced fish, shellfish, chicken and pork, plus vegetables, cooked and served in the traditional paella pan. Although there are some places on the coast that cook it well, the paella served in most tourist restaurants is frequently a formless yellow goo that does little justice to the genuine article.

A Spanish winter speciality is *cocido*, a hotpot consisting of ingredients all cooked together – meat, chicken, ham bone, sausages, vegetables, dried beans and lentils, potatoes – to make two courses: a soup with rice or noodles, then the meat and vegetables.

Tapas

It has long been a tradition in Spanish bars to serve small portions of food with each drink. The idea originated with the custom of covering glasses with a small lid or plate *(tapa)*. Someone thought to put titbits of food on these plates, perhaps to

Above: paella is the national dish

help the customers soak up the alcohol. *Tapas* were originally served free; they still are in some parts of Andalucía, but alas not on the Costa del Sol. In any case the price is never very high, and *tapas* are a great way to enjoy a 20-course meal while sampling the local specialities at different bars. *Tapas* are usually displayed under glass with prices indicated on a blackboard, so they are easy to order even if you don't speak Spanish.

A *tapa* can be as simple as a few olives, a wafer of cheese, a dollop of salad or a few marinated anchovies. One of the best choices is a slice or two of *Serrano* ham, which is salt-cured and dried in the mountain air. The best – and, at three or four times the price of other cured hams, the dearest – comes from Jabugo in the mountains of Huelva province, where it is made from free-range Ibérico pigs, which are fed on acorns.

Cooked combinations, usually served hot, display the most inventiveness. You might try kidneys in sherry sauce; octopus diced with tomato and garlic; rabbit in almond sauce; lamb stew; crisply fried fish; prawns; mussels and other shellfish (plain or with sauce); salty fried aubergines.

Wine

Spain has more land devoted to vineyards than any other country, and the quality of the wines has improved beyond recognition. Prices have increased, but Spanish wines are nevertheless excellent value for money.

Start your meal with an aperitif of chilled, dry sherry *fino*. The sherries from Jerez have long been the most important Spanish wines in terms of international prestige and exports. Córdoba's Montilla-Moriles region produces *vinos generosos* (wines with a high alcohol content) that are similar to sherry. Both of these regions produce white table wines, including Castillo de San Diego from Barbadillo in Sanlúcar de Barrameda (Cádiz), which is Spain's best-selling white.

Andalusian whites tend to be on the thin side; though very refreshing they are not strong on character. The best Spanish whites are Verdejo wines from Rueda and Albariño from Rías Baixas in Galicia. The country's wineries are currently doing some nifty things with French white grapes such as chardonnay and sauvignon blanc.

You can buy both young and aged reds (classified as *crianza*, *reserva* or *gran reserva*, depending on the time spent in the cask). Some of the best are made from Spain's tempranillo grape. Look for reds from Rioja, Ribera del Duero and Somontano. Lighter reds from the La Mancha and Valdepeñas regions have less structure and character, but are suitable as a light summer accompaniment to a meal. Spaniards often like to mix this type of wine with lemonade to make a refreshing *tinto de verano* ('summer red wine'). To end a meal, try one of Málaga's famous sweet, heavy dessert wines. Look out too for aged sweet Pedro Ximenez wines from the Montilla-Moriles region. Villages throughout Andalucía produce their own *vino del terreno* for local consumption. This usually packs quite a kick, so sample with caution. You'll find it in villages such as Manilva, Cómpeta and Frigiliana.

Hours, Etiquette and Tipping

Spain is famous for its late dining hours. However, due to the annual influx of tourists, restaurant hours on the Costa del Sol tend to be more in line with the rest of Europe. Lunch starts at any time between 1 and 3 while dinner commences at around 9pm.

To be safe, always phone ahead to book a table, especially at the better restaurants. Casual (but not sloppy) dress is acceptable at most establishments, as are children. You should be a bit smarter at the more expensive dining places, particularly for dinner.

Although service is included in the restaurant bill, it is traditional to tip the waiter around 5–10 percent. If you are paying with a credit card, it is best to tip in cash.

Price guide per head for a three course meal with house wine:
$$$ = over €36
$$ = €18–€36
$ = Under €18

Marbella

Altamirano
Plaza Altamirano 3
Tel: 952-824-932
Located in the Old Town, this is a highly popular establishment that serves excellent seafood at good prices. $

Antonio
Muelle Ribera, Puerto Banús
Tel: 952-813-536
Puerto Banús institution specialising in seafood, particularly paella. $$

Cipriano
Avenida Playas del Duque, Puerto Banús
Tel: 952-811-077
Near the Puerto Banús harbour, one of the best places in the area for fresh seafood. $$

Casa Nostra
Calle Camino José Cela 12
Tel: 952-861-108
Popular and well-run Italian restaurant. $

Don Leone
Muelle Ribera 45, Puerto Banús
Tel: 952-811-716
Fresh pasta and other Italian favourites on a summer terrace, by the wharf. $$

El Portalon
Carretera de Cadiz km185
Tel: 952-827-880
Across the street from the Marbella Club, this restaurant successfully combines the atmosphere and flavours of Castile with original creative cuisine. $$$

El Puente Romano
Hotel Puente Romano
Carretera de Cadiz, km177
Tel: 952-820-900
Especially recommended for summer dining on a terrace. Imaginative options plus Spanish and international favourites. $$$

In Vino
N340 km176, Rio Verde
Tel: 952-771-211
Fine wine is the theme of this stylish eatery. Especially pleasant when weather allows dining on the terrace. Closed Tues; dinner only in summer. $$$

La Meridiana
Camino de la Cruz s/n
Tel: 952-777-625
Located in a stunning modern palace, La Meridiana presents strikingly imaginative cuisine. Dinner only in summer. $$$

La Pesquera
Plaza de la Victoria
Tel: 952-765-170
Open all day. Informal bar/restaurant with a wide selection of seafood and grilled meats. There are several other branches of La Pesquera in and around Marbella. $

Marbella Club Grill
Carretera de Cadiz km178
Tel: 952-822-211
Fine dining in Marbella's original hotel. $$$

Red Pepper
Muelle Ribera, Puerto Banus
Tel: 952-812-148
A lively Greek taverna on the front line. $$

Santiago
Paseo Marítimo
Tel: 952-774-339
Fish and seafood restaurant with an excellent reputation. $$

Toni Dalli
Carretera de Cadiz km176
Tel: 952-770-035
A Marbella institution run by former tenor Toni Dalli, who sometimes sings for your supper. Good Italian food. Live music most nights. Dinner only. $$$

ZoZo
Plaza Altamirano 1
Tel: 952-858-868
Creative international cuisine in an atmospheric setting in an old converted house. Dinner only. Closed Sunday. $$$

West of Marbella

El Fogón de la Aldea
Urbanización La Aldea, Benahavís
Tel: 952-881-461
Grilled meats, including some of the best steak on the coast. Dinner only. $$

Iñaki Martínez
Pasaje de Torremolinos 3
San Pedro de Alcántara
Tel: 952-783-450
Traditional dishes cooked by a top Basque chef. Closed Sun. $$

eating out

La Rada
Avenida España, Estepona
Tel: 952-791-036
Fresh fish and an informal atmosphere.
Closed Wed. $

Yanx
Centro Plaza
Nueva Andalucía
Tel: 952-818-861
Café with bagels, Tex-Mex and burgers. $$

East of Marbella

El Balandro
Paseo Maritimo, Carvajal, Fuengirola
Tel: 952-661-129
Specialises in grilled red meat and roast
suckling pig. $$

Frutos
Urbanización Los Alamos
Ctra. de Cadiz km 228, Torremolinos
Tel: 952-381-450
This is a long-time favourite of many
Malagueños. No dinner Sun. $$

El Higuerón
Carretera Benalmádena-Mijas
Tel: 952-119-163
Off the motorway between Fuengirola and
Torremolinos. Housed in a 150-year-old inn,
El Higuerón serves large helpings of Span-
ish specialities. $$

La Chene Liege
La Mairena, Elviria
Tel: 952-836-092/952-852-050
A 10-minute drive into the hills to the east of
Marbella is rewarded by splendid views and
excellent French cuisine. Dinner only. $$$

La Hacienda
Urbanización Hacienda Las Chapas
Tel: 952-831-267
Long-established culinary landmark housed
in a pleasant villa. Creative Spanish and in-
ternational dishes. Closed Mon, Tues, except
in Aug; dinner only in summer. $$$

La Langosta
Francisco Cano 1, Fuengirola
Tel: 952-475-049

Long-established eatery specialising in lob-
ster dishes. Closed Sun; dinner only. $$

Moochers Jazz Café and Restaurant
Calle de la Cruz 17, Fuengirola
Tel: 952-477-154
International menu, great savoury pancakes.
Live jazz and light rock during summer. $$

Portofino
Paseo Marítimo 29, Fuengirola
Tel: 952-470-643
Italian, Spanish and international dishes.
Closed Mon; dinner only in summer. $$

Ventorrillo de la Perra
Avenida de la Constitución 115
Arroyo de la Miel
Tel: 952-441-966
An 18th-century inn near Torremolinos. Local
and international dishes. Closed Mon. $$

Inland from Marbella

Mesón El Coto
Ctra. Ronda, San Pedro de Alcántara (7km)
Tel: 952-786-688
Country inn on the road to Ronda, special-
ising in grilled meats and game dishes. $$

Refugio del Juanar
Sierra Blanca, Ojén
Tel: 952-881-000
A former hunting lodge surrounded by pine
trees in the hinterland behind Marbella.
Game dishes in season. $$

Right: alfresco dining

Taberna del Alabardero
Carretera Ronda km167
Tel: 952-812-794
Part of a chain run by a priest, the Taberna specialises in Basque cuisine. $$$

Málaga
Antonio Martín
Plaza de la Malagueta
Tel: 952-227-398
Founded at the end of the 19th century. A good place to try *fritura Malagueña*. $$

Bar Logueno
Calle Marin Garcia
No phone
Well-loved traditional *tapas* bar. $

Café de París
Velez Málaga 8
Tel: 952-225-043
Creative cuisine. Closed Mon. $$$

Chinitas
Moreno Monroy 4
Tel: 952-210-972
Classic regional cuisine. $$

Parador de Gibralfaro
Monte de Gibralfaro
Tel: 952-221-902
Fine Spanish and international cuisine and unbeatable views over the bay. $$

Ronda
Hotel Don Miguel
Plaza de España
Tel: 952-877-722

Traditional Spanish cuisine. Terraces with views of Ronda's Puente Viejo bridge. $$

Parador de Ronda
Plaza de España
Tel: 952-877-500
Local, regional and international dishes. $$$

Pedro Romero
Virgen de la Paz 18
Tel: 952-871-110
Traditional Andalusian dishes. *Rabo de toro* (braised bulls tails) is a speciality. $$

Tragabuches
Calle José Aparicio 1
Tel: 952-190-291
Innovative renditions of classic Andalusian dishes. Closed Sun evening and Mon. $$$

Antequera
El Angelote
Plaza Coso Viejo
Tel: 952-703-465
Andalusian cuisine. Closed Mon. $$

Lozano
Avenida Principal 2, Poligono Industrial
Tel: 952-842-712
Good food at reasonable prices. $$

Parador de Antequera
Garcia del Olmo
Tel: 952-840-261
With views over the Antequera valley. $$

Nerja
Casa Luque
Plaza Cavana 2
Tel: 952-521-004
Northern Spain cuisine. Closed Wed. $$$

Pepe Rico
Almirante Ferrandiz 28
Tel: 952-520-247
Spanish and Scandinavian inspired food. $$

La Fonda
Calle Cristo 35
Tel: 952-524-974
Andalusian specialities. $$

Left: dish of the day

NIGHTLIFE

Clubs

Marbella's famed nightlife revolves around its many bars and clubs. An evening out can consist of a round of *tapas* taverns in the old part of Marbella, or dancing to music at one of the trendy bars that are so plentiful in the country's most hedonistic resort.

If you're looking for nightlife hot spots, Puerto Banús is the place to be. People meet at bars such as Sinatra or Salduba, at the entrance to the harbour, to decide on their next move. Nightlife venues go in and out of fashion from one season to the next. Marbella is quite fickle in this respect, but some of the steady favourites include La Comedia, News Café, Old Joy's Pub and The Navy Club.

If you're after something more sedate or sophisticated, head inland from Puerto Banús and sample the scene at la Notte (tel: 952-776-190), a piano bar that adjoins La Meridina restaurant.

The most renowned disco scene is at the exclusive Olivia Valere club (tel: 952-828-861) on Carretera de Istán, which is popular with film stars and sheikhs. Somewhat more casual is Oh! Marbella (tel: 952-835-477) in the Hotel Don Carlos, some 10km (6 miles) east of the centre of Marbella.

During the summer months much of the action shifts to Marbella's beach clubs, such as the Babaloo Beach. Many organise regular theme parties at which revellers dance the night away. One of the more exclusive beachside venues is the Café del Mar, in the Hotel Puente Romano.

Further along the coast you will find exciting nightlife centres at the Puerto de Benalmadena marina and in Torremolinos, where there is an active gay scene.

Many of the bars in Puerto Banús and Marbella feature live music some days of the week, as do a handful of clubs in Málaga. In summer there are concerts and theatre performances at the auditorium in the Parque de la Constitución in central Marbella, and at several other venues around town. However, internationally known acts tend to appear in Málaga, at the city's Teatro Cervantes (tel: 952-224-100) or, when it comes to major rock concerts, the Málaga bullring.

Flamenco

Though the roots of flamenco are found in Moorish songs, the tradition was adopted by Spanish gypsies as the musical expression of an impoverished and often oppressed race. The pinnacle of the true flamenco singer's art is the body of great songs known as *cante jondo* ('deep song'). In its multitude of variants, *cante jondo* features wailing lyrics that speak of passion and suffering, to the accompaniment of a guitar and rhythmic clapping.

Pure *cante jondo* is a minority art that is inaccessible even to most Spaniards. At its best, it is seen in the private *peñas* (flamenco clubs, the most famous of which are in

Jerez), or in the summer flamenco festivals held in villages of the Andalusian hinterland.

The *tablaos* (flamenco shows) on the Costa del Sol present a diluted version that focuses on the lighter, more flowery form of flamenco. Although purists frown on these spectacles as travesties of the real thing, for a rollicking show of boisterous singing, clapping, and thunderous foot-stomping dances, an evening at one of the flamenco clubs on the coast can be a lot of fun. It will also give you an insight into this uniquely Andalusian art form.

Flamenco Ana María

Plaza de Santo Cristo 4–5
Marbella
Tel: 952-775-646/860-704
The traditional Marbella venue for flamenco shows. The curtain rises at around 11pm.

Above: young clubbers in Torremolinos

Bona Dea
Calle 2B, Las Yedras
Plaza Las Dalias
Nueva Andalucía
Tel: 952-816-044)
Bona Dea offers a flamenco spectacle with gourmet dinner. Dinner is from 9pm, and the show starts at 11pm.

Taberna Flamenca Pepe Lopez
Tel: 952-381-284
Located on Torremolinos's Plaza de la Gamba Alegre, this is one of several long-established flamenco clubs on the coast.

Casinos
Formal dress and possession of a passport or other form of identification are required to gain access to the coast's gambling casinos. All offer roulette, blackjack and other table games, plus slot machines.

Casino Marbella
Hotel Nueva Andalucía
Nueva Andalucía, Marbella
Tel: 952-814-000
Slot machines available from 4pm, gaming room from 8pm.

Casino Torrequebrada
N340 km220
Benalmádena-Costa
Tel: 952-446-000
Gaming rooms open at 9pm. Live show in the Fortuna Nightclub starts at 10.30pm.

Casino de San Roque
Carretera N340 km127, San Roque
Tel: 965-780-100
The coast's newest casino, past Sotogrande. Gaming room opens at 8pm.

Cinema
Complejo Cinematográfico, Gran Marbella
Puerto Banús
Tel: 952-810-077
A modern complex with eight theatres, one of which screens recent releases in English.

Attractions
Escuela de Arte Ecuestre
N340 km159, Estepona
Tel: 952-808-077
Horse centre, with dressage show on Friday evenings in summer, Tuesdays in winter.

Garden of Eagles
Benalmádena
Tel: 952-568-239
Entertaining birds of prey show and falconry display.

Hipódromo Costa del Sol
Urbanización El Chaparral, Mijas-Costa
Tel: 952-592-700
To the west of Fuengirola, the coast's horse-racing track stages regular races during winter, and occasional evening races in summer.

Sealife
Puerto Marina, Benalmádena
Tel: 952-560-150
An aquariumn located in the Benalmádena sports harbour. Features a variety of fish life, with the highlight being a large shark tank.

Selwo
N340 km162.5
Estepona
Tel: 952-792-150
A 100-hectare (250-acre) wildlife park with lions, tigers, elephants, giraffes and many more wild species.

Tivoli World
Arrogu de la Miel
Tel: 952-257-016
Amusement park with over two dozen rides, regular shows, several restaurants and bars.

Left: flamenco dancing

CALENDAR OF EVENTS

The local calendar is dotted with *fiestas*, *ferias* and *romerías*. A *fiesta* often celebrates a saint's day or a similar religious event; the previous night features music and dancing. Floats form a procession through the streets and there is frequently an open-air Mass. *Ferias* are week-long communal parties. *Romerías* are pilgrimages to a religious shrine in the country.

A number of shops and restaurants close in August, when most of Spain is on holiday.

January

Cabalgata de los Reyes (5–6th): float parades, the Three Wise Men disperse sweeties to the crowds, and distribute gifts to children. Saints feast days – St Anthony in Mijas and Nerja, St Sebastián in Casabermeja.

February

Carnaval, banned under Franco; revived as a pre-Lenten outburst of indulgence.

March / April

Semana Santa (Easter Week) sees Spain return to the Dark Ages. Images of the Virgin and Christ are carried on richly ornate *pasos* (floats) by members of various brotherhoods. Hooded *penitentes*, some with feet in chains, walk ahead. Only shuffling feet, tinkling bells, banging drums and the occasional *saeta* (devotional song) break the silence; thousands of candles light the darkness. Each village and town has its own procession. It is worth making a trip to Seville for the *Feria de Abril* (starting two weeks after Easter), for the country's most exuberant spring festival.

May

On **Cruces de Mayo** (3rd), neighbourhoods compete to form the best procession with crosses decorated with paper flowers. Children re-enact *Semana Santa* (holy week). **Corpus Christi** (sometimes in June) sees more processions along streets covered with petals and sweet-smelling herbs.

June

In the week of the 11th, Marbella's *Fiesta de San Bernabé* marks the town's conquest by the Catholic monarchs with a procession.

Día de San Juan (24th) is a national day of recovery from the previous night's celebrations, which involved bonfires and effigies of Judas burned at the stake. There are noisy fireworks displays.

July

Virgen del Carmen (16th) honours the patroness of fishermen through boat processions. Events in Estepona, Fuengirola, Málaga and Nerja are among the biggest in the country.

August

Feria de Málaga, celebrated during the first fortnight, emulates Seville's Spring Fair.

September

Feria y Fiesta de Pedro Romero (first fortnight) features, in addition to the usual party atmosphere, major bullfighting events that include the *Corrida Goyesca* (Goyaesque bullfight) in early 19th-century costumes.

October

Feria y Romería del Rosario. In the first full week, Fuengirola has a big *feria* and a *romería* to a field off the N340 where a model of the Virgin's shrine is mounted.

Saint's Day in San Pedro de Alcántara (19th) is celebrated with an open-air Mass and a procession.

December

Traditional Malaga folk-musicians compete in a contest at the Venta de San Cayetano, Puerto de la Torre (28th)

Above: villagers on horseback celebrate a local *fiesta*.

Practical
Information

TRAVEL ESSENTIALS

Orientation

Marbella stretches for 26km (16 miles) along Spain's Costa del Sol. It is in Málaga province – one of Andalucía's eight provinces. Andalucía, one of Spain's 17 'autonomous communities', has Seville as its capital. Marbella's resident population is just under 100,000.

Málaga city, the provincial capital, has around 500,000 inhabitants. The N340 (E15) dual carriageway coastal highway runs west from Málaga for 56km (35 miles) to Marbella, passing Málaga airport 7km (4 miles) from the city centre. There is an alternative toll motorway (A7) from Fuengirola, east of Marbella, to Estopona in the west. Seville is 220km (137 miles) northwest of Málaga; Córdoba is 185km (115 miles) north; Granada is 130km (81 miles) to the northeast.

When it comes to the clock, Spain is in line with the majority of European countries: in summer it is two hours ahead of GMT; in winter, one hour ahead.

Andalusians speak Castilian Spanish with some local variations. The number of natives who speak other languages is limited, so if you don't have a command of Spanish, you might consider buying one of the phrase books that are available at many outlets.

Climate and Clothing

The climate on the Costa del Sol is typically Mediterranean – summers are hot, winters (when most of what rain there is falls) are relatively mild, and spring and autumn both have agreeable weather.

The Sierra Blanca behind Marbella gives the city a microclimate that is a little cooler than most of the south coast in summer and a little warmer in winter.

The average temperature is 18°C (64°F) and there is an annual average of 320 days of sunshine. In the summer temperatures may exceed 30°C (86°F); in winter they rarely drop below 12°C (54°F). Loose-fitting cotton clothes are therefore an obvious choice for summer; add light sweaters for spring and autumn, and slightly heavier layers plus a light raincoat and maybe an umbrella in winter. Marbella is fashion-conscious but the style is casual.

When to Go

Any time of year is good for a visit to Spain's Costa del Sol. The summer season, when restaurants, hotels, discos and the like are in full swing, is from mid-June to the end of September. In winter, however, you will find bargains in both car hire and accommodation. Winter is probably the best season for golfers. Most nature-lovers will appreciate the glorious springtime display.

GETTING THERE

By Air

Flying to Málaga airport on scheduled or charter services, possibly with an accommodation package, is the most popular way of getting to the Costa del Sol. The airport's capacity has recently doubled to 11 million passengers per year and there are many more intercontinental services. Seville, Jerez de la Frontera and Gibraltar are other points of arrival by air.

Travel agents will have the latest information on flights and package availability. Málaga has the usual facilities of a Grade 1

Left: Puerto Banús marina in Marbella
Right: Spain's new motorway system

international airport, including excellent duty-free shopping. There is a regular bus service to Marbella. Check the current taxi fare to Marbella at the information desk before leaving the airport; take only registered taxis and agree the fare in advance. For flight arrivals, tel: 952 048 838; flight departures, tel: 952 048 804

By Road
Drivers head for Málaga and then Marbella along Spain's fast-improving road network. It is apparently possible to drive from Rome, Copenhagen or London without being stopped by traffic lights, which doesn't mean that there aren't Civil Guard motorcycle patrolmen around, who can administer heavy, on-the-spot fines for driving offences. For information, you should consult motoring organisations in your home country. Driving is on the right and seatbelts are obligatory.

By Rail
Málaga is the Costa del Sol's main railway terminus (tel: 952-360-202). Here again, major improvements in the infrastructure have improved services. Renfe is the national rail operator and its *talgo* trains are the best. Travel agents can provide information about routes, times and fare schemes.

By Sea
Cruise liners regularly call at Málaga and a scheduled Trasmediterránea service connects with Barcelona and the Canary Islands.
Marbella's three marinas are at:
● Puerto Banús (tel: 952-814-750)
● Puerto de Marbella (tel: 952-775-700)
● Puerto Cabopino (tel: 952-831-975).

Documents
Citizens of EU countries require a national identity card or passport, but not a visa. Citizens of some other countries, such as the United States, Australia and many Latin American states, do not need visas for stays of up to 90 days. South African citizens need a visa. All non-EU citizens need a passport. If in doubt, check with the Spanish consulate in your country. Medical certificates are not required of people arriving from most parts of the world. National driving licences from most countries are valid.

Customs Regulations
Duty-free allowances for non-European Union travellers to Spain are: 200 cigarettes (or 50 cigars), 1 litre of alcohol, 2 litres of wine, ¼ litre of eau-du-cologne and 50 grams of perfume. There is no duty-free allowance for those travelling between EU countries.

Any amount of local or foreign currency can be imported, but if you are travelling with over €3000 this should be declared to customs. Please note, customs officers are very vigilant.

Electricity
Spain uses AC at 220 volts, 50hz. Plugs have two round pins. Remember to pack a plug adapter and a transformer if you are bringing 110V appliances on your trip.

MONEY MATTERS

Spain is one of 12 European Union countries to use a single currency, the Euro (€). Coins are issued in denominations of 1, 2, 5, 10, 20, and 50 cents and 1 and 2 Euros. Notes are issued in denominations of 5, 10, 20, 50, 100, 200 and 500 Euros.

All major credit and charge cards are accepted, but Visa is the most common card. There are many ATMs at which credit cards and some foreign-issued bank cards can be used to obtain money – as long as you remember your PIN number.

Banks, which are plentiful, are the best places to exchange currency. They open Mon–Fri 9am–2pm, Sat 9am–1pm (in summer banks are closed Saturday). There are also many *Cajas de Cambio* (bureaux de change), which operate longer opening hours. These tend to offer a poorer rate of exchange than banks, but often don't charge commission.

Tax
IVA, a value-added tax, applies on most goods and services at the rate of 7 percent. On goods and services that are considered luxuries including things like car hire and camera film, this rises to 16 percent. If you have resident status in a non-EU country and want to make a purchase of more than €90, you might be eligible for exemption from IVA.

practical information

ACCOMMODATION

Hotels are officially rated from one up to five stars, though there is also a rating of five stars-plus *gran lujo*, which indicates a level of opulent luxury. *Hostales* are awarded one to three stars. *Pensiónes* have one or two stars. Officially classified tourist apartments (ATs) have one to three keys.

If you're looking for private lettings or specialist villa and apartment holiday firms, it's a good idea to consult the travel pages of newspapers in your home country for relevant advertisements before you set out.

Marbella has an exceptional range of top-rated hotels. The choice in the less expensive categories is more limited. The price codes in the following listings are based on a double room in high season.

$$$ = over €150
$$ = €60–€90
$ = €60

Marbella
★★★★★
Gran Melia Don Pepe
José Melia s/n
Tel: 952-770-300
Fax: 952-779-954
Email: gran.melia.don.pepe@solmelia.com
Located at the western end of the town, in close proximity to the beach, Gran Melia Don Pepe is one of the oldest and most venerable of Marbella's hotels. In addition to being luxurious and impeccably maintained, it is one of the resort's most convenient hotels for the town centre. 202 rooms. $$$

Los Monteros
Carretera de Cadiz km187
Tel: 952-771-700
Fax: 952-823-721
Email: hotel@monteros.com
This is the perfect choice for sports enthusiasts. Los Monteros includes the Río Real golf course, a tennis club with 10 courts, and five squash courts. There is a variety of water sports at La Cabane Beach Club. The actual accommodation is in rooms decorated with different regional themes within three pavilions surrounded by gardens. There is a choice of two restaurants. 177 rooms. $$$

Puente Romano
Carretera de Cadiz km177
Tel: 952-820-900
Fax: 952-775-766
Email: reservas@puenteromano.com
This Moorish *pueblo*-style complex is surrounded by luxuriant trees, shrubs, flowers and lawns that are tended by a small army of gardeners. Rooms are luxurious by any standards. The El Puente and La Plaza restaurants overlook the Roman bridge after which the hotel is named. There is a tennis club, two pools, and arrangements with three golf clubs. 274 rooms. $$$

★★★★
Coral Beach
Carretera de Cadiz km176
Tel: 952-868-771
Fax: 952-857-995
Email: reservas@hotelcoralbeach.com
Fringed by palm trees, right on the beach in the heart of Marbella's Golden Mile, the Coral Beach has two restaurants plus a beach club and health centre. 170 rooms. Open Mar–Nov. $$$

Hotel El Fuerte
Avenida El Fuerte
Tel: 952-861-500
Fax: 952-824-411
Email: elfuerte@fuertehoteles.com
Hotel El Fuerte is a pleasant, classic estab-

lishment, and, of all Marbella's many top-class hotels, it enjoys what is probably the optimum central location – near the sea at the eastern end of the Paseo Marítimo. 250 rooms. $$

Above: holiday makers enjoy one of the Hotel Puente Romano's two pools

Marbella Club Hotel
Carretera de Cadiz 178
Marbella
Tel: 952-822-211
Fax: 952-829-884
Email: reservas@marbellaclub.com
This is where today's Costa del Sol all started in the 1950s, and this legendary hotel still exudes the atmosphere of an exclusive club. The Marbella Club Hotel has stylishly appointed suites, bungalows and rooms, all set out in a subtropical garden. Public rooms are cosily luxurious, and there is a restaurant, beach club, two pools and a fitness centre. 126 rooms and 10 bungalows. $$$

Riu Rincón Andaluz
Carretera de Cadiz km173
Tel: 952-811-517
Fax: 952-814-180
The pretty Riu Rincón Andaluz is modelled on an Andalusian *pueblo* (village), and is surrounded by luxury villas. Near the sea and close to Puerto Banús. 315 rooms. $$

★★
Lima
Avenida Belón 2
Tel: 952-770-500
Fax: 952-863-091
Email: limahotel@terra.es
Conveniently located in central Marbella, just one block from the Paseo Marítimo. The Lima is a comfortable choice, if somewhat old-fashioned, and is a good mid-range bet. 64 rooms. $

Hostels
Enriqueta
Calle Los Caballeros
Tel: 952-827-552
A small, simple hostel in an excellent location not far from the Plaza de los Naranjos. 20 rooms. $

El Castillo
Plaza San Bernabé 2
Tel: 952-771-739
Well located next to the Old Town, El Castillo has basic, tasteful, clean rooms for a mostly young clientele. 26 rooms. $

Apartments
Jardines del Mar
Paraje Don Pepe
Tel: 952-776-000
Comfortable two-room apartments set in pleasant gardens. $$

Benabola Park Plaza
Puerto Banús
Tel: 952-815-068
Fax: 952-812-846
Apartments for up to six people in the heart of the port. $$

West of Marbella
★★★★★
Kempinski
Playa El Padrón
Carretera de Cadiz km159
Estepona
Tel: 952-809-500
Fax: 952-809-550
Email: agp.reservation@kempinski.com
Deluxe resort on the beach a few miles east of Estepona town centre. Four pools (one indoor) and a fitness centre. 149 rooms. $$$

Las Dunas
La Boladilla Baja
Carretera de Cadiz km163.5
Estepona
Tel: 952-794-345
Fax: 952-794-825
Email: lasdunas@accor.com
Luxurious spa hotel with fitness centre and health programmes, located right next to the beach, about halfway between Estepona and Marbella. 73 rooms and 33 apartments. $$$

Left: a child's paradise

★★★★
Atalaya Park
Carretera de Cadiz km168.5
Estepona
Tel: 952-889-000
Fax: 952-889-022
Email: hotel@atalayapark.es
A sprawling hotel not far from San Pedro
de Alcántara set amidst gardens near the sea.
Golf course, five swimming pools, three
restaurants, and tennis courts. 489 rooms
and 15 bungalows. $$$

El Paraiso
Urbanización El Paraiso
Carretera de Cadiz km167
Estepona
Tel: 952-883-000
Fax: 952-882-019
Email: hparaiso@jet.es
Located on a hilltop surrounded by golf
courses, with wonderful views of the Medi-
terranean. Fitness centre. 175 rooms. $$$

Golf Hotel Guadalmina
Urbanización Guadalmina Baja
San Pedro de Alcántara
Tel: 952-882-211
Fax: 952-882-291
Email: reservas@hotelguadalmina.com
Set in a tranquil location by the beach, and
surrounded by golf courses and gardens.
Close to the town of San Pedro and Puerto
Banús. 177 rooms. $$

★★★
Amanhavis
Calle Pilar 3
Benahavís
Tel: 952-856-026
Fax: 952-856-151
Email: info@amanhavis.com
Beautiful modern Moorish fantasy palace in
the delightful village of Benahavís. Each
suite is decorated with a different theme re-
lating to Spanish medieval history. $$

Diana Park
Carretera de Cadiz km168.5
Estepona
Tel: 952-887-659
Fax: 952-884-279
Email: comercial@hoteldianapark.com

Pleasant, modern hotel set midway between
Estepona and Marbella, with access to many
sports facilities. Beach club. 90 rooms. $$

Hotel La Cartuja
Campos de la Cartuja
Carretera Benahavís km1.5
Tel: 952-882-270
Fax: 952-882-086
Stylish hotel overlooking the Atalaya golf
course, just inland from the sea. A variety of
suites and self-catering apartments, pools,
sports facilities and a good restaurant. $$

★★
Albero Lodge
Carretera de Cadiz km164.5
Calle Tamesis 15
Finca La Cancelada
Estepona
Tel: 952-880-700
Fax: 952-885-238
Email: info@alberolodge.com
Delightful, stylish nine-room hotel set in a
converted villa not far from the beach, and
surrounded by gardens. $$

East of Marbella
★★★★★
Byblos Andaluz
Urbanización Mijas-Golf
Mijas Costa, Málaga
Tel: 952-473-050
Fax: 952-476-783
Email: comercial@byblos-andaluz.com
An Andalusian-style spa hotel, and the per-
fect choice for anyone who wants to pamper
themselves in palatial splendour. It adjoins
a golf course and its health centre offers tha-
lassotherapy treatments (based on sea wa-
ter), massage, and so forth. 144 rooms. $$$

Don Carlos
Carretera de Cadiz km192
Marbella
Tel: 952-831-140
Fax: 952-833-429
Email: info@hoteldoncarlos.com
Rising high above the pine woods, near the
beach about 11km (7 miles) to the east of
central Marbella, the Don Carlos hotel fea-
tures a tennis club, beach club and the lively
Oh! Marbella disco. $$$

La Cala Resort
La Cala de Mijas
Mijas-Costa
Tel: 952-669-000
Fax: 952-669-039
Email: lacala@lacala.com
The atmosphere at the stylish La Cala Resort is refreshingly relaxed. Not only is the hotel surrounded by golf courses, but its large rooms' picture windows overlook some of the fairways. 107 rooms. $$$

★★★
Hotel Mijas
Urbanización Tamisa
Mijas
Tel: 952-485-800
Fax: 952-485-825
Email: mijasres@hotasa.es
This modern, airy hotel with lovely ample gardens is on the periphery of the picture-postcard village of Mijas, and has some of the best views on the coast. 204 rooms. $$

Inland from Marbella
★★★
Castillo de Monda
Monda
Tel: 952-457-142
Fax: 952-457-336
Email: mondas@spa.es
On a hilltop overlooking the village of Monda, the Castillo de Monda incorporates the remains of the original fortress, and, in keeping with the location, is designed as a Moorish style castle, with the interior décor following the theme. 23 rooms. $$

Refugio del Juanar
Sierra Blanca
Ojén
Tel: 952-881-000
Fax: 952-881-001
Email: juanar@sopde.es
The Refugio del Juanar is a rustic mountain retreat in a former royal hunting lodge right in the middle of a forest in the mountains just inland from Marbella. The Marqués of Larios had the building constructed for his hunting parties. The hotel is now operated by a workers' co-operative. In season, the restaurant serves delicious game dishes. 26 rooms. $$

GETTING AROUND

By Car
The biggest international car hire firms are represented in Marbella and also at Málaga airport, but it may be cheaper to organise your transport before arriving in Spain. Some airlines have 'fly-drive' packages. You might find companies advertising budget car rentals in the travel pages of newspapers in your home country. Some 40 local firms generally have better rates than the big operators. Four local firms to try are:

Niza Car Interrent
Calle Alonso de Bazán, Marbella.
Tel: 952-770-931
Fax: 952-771-352

Rual
N340, km178
San Pedro de Alcántara
Tel: 952-780-408
Fax: 952-786-890

Helle Hollis
Calle Camilo José Cela 21
Marbella
Tel: 952-823-038
Fax: 952-822-711

ATA
Adva. Ricardo soriano
Marbella
Tel: 952-828-637

Although the rules of the road are much the same as in the rest of Western Europe, Spain suffers from a much higher than average road accident and death rate. Eccentric (to say nothing of bad) driving is a hazard.

The N340 dual carriageway is the main road along the coast. Inland, the A7 motorway runs from Málaga to Estepona and beyond. This is a toll highway in two of its sections (from Fuengirola to the eastern end of Marbella, and from the western end of Marbella to Estepona). If you overshoot

our destination, look for a *Cambio de Sentido* sign, at which you can do a U-turn.

Car hire firms ought to notify you of the procedure in case of accident or breakdown. If you are in your own car, your travel or car-insurance company might issue special instructions and organise the arrangements. You may need to get a *grua* (towing truck) and find a *taller de reparaciones* (repair shop). In many cases foreign motoring organisations have reciprocal arrangements with the Real Automóvil Club de España, calle Córdoba 17, Málaga (tel: 952-229-836).

Gasolineras (petrol stations) sell super (97 octane), unleaded (*sin plomo* 96 and 98), and *gas oil* (diesel). Most stations are open 24 hours a day.

By Bus and Taxi

There are three urban bus routes in Marbella: Plaza de Toros through the centre to the Costa Marbella shopping centre; Centre through Albarizas to Hotel Don Miguel; Centre to Club de Fútbol and to Miraflores. From the bus terminal on Avenida Trapiche there is a spreading network of regular services along the Costa del Sol and to inland villages, towns and cities. The buses are comfortable and fares very reasonable.

Taxis are plentiful and relatively cheap. Agree on the fare in advance on longer trips. The rates are fixed on most journeys.

COMMUNICATIONS AND MEDIA

Keeping in Touch

Post offices *(Correos)* open Mon–Fri 9am–2pm, also Sat 9am–1pm at Jacinto Behavente 14, Marbella (tel: 952-772-898), and calle Pizarro, San Pedro de Alcántara (tel: 952-780-393).

To phone abroad, dial the international access code 00, then the country code:

Australia (61)
France (33)
Germany (49)
Italy (39)
Japan (81)
Netherlands (31)
United Kingdom (44)
US and Canada (1)

If you are using a US credit phone card, dial the company's access number, then 00, and then the country code: Sprint: 900-990-013; AT&T: 900-990-011; MCI: 900-990-014.

In the UK, the numbers are: BT: 900-990-044; Mercury: 900-990-944.

Media

The Málaga daily newspaper *Sur* publishes a free English-language edition on Fridays. *Absolute Marbella* is a colour glossy devoted to Marbella lifestyle. *Die Aktuelle* covers the Costa del Sol in German. *Solkysten* does the same for Scandinavians. Several radio stations broadcast in English, including the Marbella-based OCI (101.6 FM). Billboards and flyers also publicise special events.

Other useful sources of information on the latest in local entertainment include hotels and clubs, which are all too happy to promote their area.

HOURS AND HOLIDAYS

Business Hours

Most business are open Mon–Sat 9 or 10am–1.30 or 2pm, then, following the siesta hours, 4 or 5pm–8 or 9pm. A number of shops do not reopen on Saturday afternoons; some supermarkets and department stores stay open later. On Sundays and public holidays, you should find a number of supermarkets and tourist shops plying their wares.

Public Holidays

In addition to local *fiestas* (June 11, Oct 19 in Marbella) and the changeable dates of the Easter holidays, public holidays in Andalucía are as follows:

1	January	Año Nuevo
6	January	Día de los Reyes
28	February	Día de Andalucía
1	May	Día del Trabajo
15	August	Asunción
12	October	Hispanidad (Columbus Day)
1	November	Todos los Santos
6	December	Constitution Day
8	December	Inmaculada Concepción
25	December	Navidad (Christmas)

EMERGENCIES

Police

The *Policia Nacional* (tel: 091) deals with Spain's internal security and with law and order in the main urban areas. Its members are easily distinguishable by their navy blue uniforms. To call its HQ, tel: 952-771-193.

The *Guardia Civil* (tel: 062) is responsible for law and order on the coast, in outlying towns and in rural areas. Its members wear green uniforms. Its HQs are at Plaza Leganitos in Marbella (tel: 952-771-399), and Playa del Ancón, San Pedro de Alcántara (tel: 952-771-944). It also runs the highway patrol from Marbella's calle San Antonio (tel: 952-772-549).

The *Policia Local* (tel: 092), in blue but with checked bands, are mainly responsible for urban traffic control and civil protection. Its offices are at Juan De La Cierva, Marbella (tel: 952-827-589) and at Avenida Marqués del Duero 68, San Pedro de Alcántara (tel: 952-783-099).

Robbery

Thefts from cars or from private or hotel accommodation are not unknown, and mugging has also become a public hazard in the main cities. The need to feed a drug dependence is the motivation for many street villains, especially in cities such as Málaga and Seville. Take sensible precautions, as you would anywhere, and be discreet with valuables such as wallets and jewellery. Don't leave valuables lying around your hotel room when you are not there.

Accident and Sickness

If you reside in an EU country whose national health services provide E110, E111 or E112 forms, you should benefit from reciprocal arrangements with SAS, Andalucía's public health service, which is generally excellent. However, you will need to have filled in the forms in advance of your visit.. In any case, to cover all eventualities, it is best to take out private health insurance.

The SAS Centro de Salud (Health Centre; tel: 952-772-184) is on Plaza Leganitos, and the general hospital (Hospital Comarcal; tel: 952-862-748) is just east of the town.

Marbella has a very large population of *medicos* (doctors) in all the specialised fields. There are also a number of private clinics from which you can obtain local advice and recommendations. The private Marbella Clinic (tel: 952-774-200) is on the town's eastern edge opposite the *gasolinera*.

Pharmacies *(Farmacias)* are identified by green or red crosses and can often advise and deal directly with minor ailments. Outside normal shopping hours they display the name and address of the nearest *farmacia de guardia* which will be open.

Emergency Numbers

National Police Tel: 091
Local Police Tel: 092
Municipal Ambulance for Marbella Tel: 952-772-749
Red Cross *(Cruz Roja)* Tel: 952-774 534/ 861-688
Fire Brigade *(Bomberos)* Tel: 952-774-349

SPORT

Golf

There are 11 golf courses within the town boundaries of Marbella, and more within a short travelling distance. Non-members can have difficulty in getting a game during weekends and school holidays. One solution is to settle for inconvenient starting times, such as very early in the morning or in the midday sun on hot summer days.

Premier hotels have arrangements with particular courses but this doesn't necessarily help with booking a game at a convenient time. The best advice is to book a starting time well in advance through your hotel's concierge or direct with the club. High demand means that green fees are relatively high – check them out in advance. In order to play a round, you need to bring your handicap card from your home club.

All the clubs have professional coaches, and golf clubs and cart rentals for hire. Most also rent out buggies. All have a bar and restaurant and most have a swimming pool and tennis courts. Málaga's provincial tourist board publishes relevant information, or see *Andalucía Golf* and *Sun Golf* – both of which are informative local publications.

Tennis

Most of Marbella's top hotels have excellent tennis facilities; hotel guests have court-rental priority. You have to be either a guest or a member to play at the top-notch **Puente Romano Tennis and Fitness Club** (tel: 952-820-900). Other hotels with good facilities include the Hotel Los Monteros (tel: 952-771-700), with 10 quick-surface courts, and the Hotel Don Carlos (tel: 952-831-140)

Tennis clubs include El Madroñal Club (tel: 952-785-307), 7km (4 miles) down the San Pedro to Ronda road, and the Club de Tenis El Casco (tel: 952-837-651) in Urbanización El Rosario, east of Marbella.

Horse Riding

The country inland is ideal for horse trekking. Horse-riding centres include: Picador La Granja, Camino de los Molinos, Ronda, tel: 952-875-956; Hurricane Hotel, Tarifa, tel: 956-684-919; Elviria Equestrian Centre, Las Chapas, between Marbella and Fuengirola, tel: 952-835-272; Hipica International, calle Hurriana, tel: 952-625-217.

USEFUL INFORMATION

Tourist Offices in UK and US

22–3 Manchester Square, London W1M 5AP, tel: 020-7486 8077; fax: 020-7486 8034; www.tourspain.co.uk.
666 Fifth Avenue, New York, NY 10103, tel: 212-265 8822, fax: 212-265 8864; www.okspain.org.

Tourist Offices in Spain

Marbella: Plaza de los Naranjos, tel: 952-823-550; Glorieta de la Fontanilla, tel: 952-771-442. **San Pedro de Alcántara**: Avenida Marqués del Duero, tel: 952-785-252. **Málaga**, Avda Cervantes, tel: 952-604-410; Pasaje de Chinitas, tel: 952-213-445. www.marbella.es.

Consulates (Consulados)

Many countries maintain local consulates, primarily in Málaga. Police, tourist offices and hotels can provide addresses and phone numbers. These include: Germany: 952-212-442; UK: 952-352-300; USA: 952-474-891; Canada: 952-223-346.

FURTHER READING

Travel Information

Insight Guide: Southern Spain (Apa Publications). A detailed account of the region's history, culture and people with an emphasis on sights and activities for visitors, accompanied by superlative photography and maps.
Insight Pocket Guide: Southern Spain (Apa Publications). A concise introduction to both the wonders and the practical details of the area, complete with pull-out map.

Culture

Death in the Afternoon, by Ernest Hemingway (Cape). The American novelist's account of the bullfifght. Maligned by purists but an informative and gripping read.
In Search of the Firedance, by James Woodall (Sinclair Stevenson). Everything you need to know about flamenco and its origins.

Food and Wine

Cooking in Spain, by Janet Mendel (Santana). Encyclopaedic volume on Spanish cookery with 400 recipes and colourful insights into local cuisine.
Encyclopaedia of Spanish and Portuguese Wine, by Kathryn McWhirter and Charles Metcalfe (Simon & Schuster). A fine introduction to the new Iberian wines.

Right: fine horse-riding country

ACKNOWLEDGEMENTS

2/3, 51	**J. D Dallet**
1, 8/9, 21, 22T/B, 24, 33, 46, 52, 53T, 57, 60B, 69, 71, 72	**Jerry Dennis**
10	**Andrew Eames**
16, 23, 25, 27T, 29, 30, 32B, 36, 37B, 40, 41T/B, 42, 45, 47, 50, 55, 58, 65, 83, 86	**Jens Poulsen**
15B	**Jan Read**
5, 6T/b, 7T/B, 15T, 20, 27b, 28, 31, 32T, 35T/B, 37T, 39T/b, 44, 49, 53B, 54, 56T/B, 59, 60T, 61, 63T/B, 66, 67, 68, 75, 77, 78, 79, 80, 84, 87, 89, 90	**Mark Read**
62	**Real Escuela Andaluza del Arte Ecuestre**
11, 64	**Bill Wassman**
Front cover	**Steve Allen/Photographer's Choice/Getty Images**
Original cartography	**Berndtson & Berndtson**

© APA Publications GmbH & Co. Verlag KG Singapore Branch, Singapore

Left: a festive *paseo* in full swing

INSIGHT
Pocket Guides

Insight Pocket Guides pioneered a new approach to guidebooks, introducing the concept of the authors as "local hosts" who would provide readers with personal recommendations, just as they would give honest advice to a friend who came to stay. They also included a full-size pull-out map. Now, to cope with the needs of the 21st century, new editions in this growing series are being given a new look to make them more practical to use, and restaurant and hotel listings have been greatly expanded.

Also from Insight Guides...

Insight Guides is the classic series, providing the complete picture with expert and informative text and stunning photography. Each book is an ideal travel planner, a reliable on-the-spot companion – and a superb visual souvenir of a trip. 193 titles.

Insight Maps are designed to complement the guidebooks. They provide full mapping of major destinations, and their laminated finish gives them ease of use and durability. 100 titles.

Insight Compact Guides are handy reference books, modestly priced yet comprehensive. The text, pictures and maps are all cross-referenced, making them ideal books to consult while seeing the sights. 127 titles.

INSIGHT POCKET GUIDE TITLES

Aegean Islands
Algarve
Alsace
Amsterdam
Athens
Atlanta
Bahamas
Baja Peninsula
Bali
Bali Bird Walks
Bangkok
Barbados
Barcelona
Bavaria
Beijing
Berlin
Bermuda
Bhutan
Boston
Brisbane & the
   Gold Coast
British Columbia
Brittany
Brussels
Budapest
California,
   Northern

Canton
Cape Town
Chiang Mai
Chicago
Corfu
Corsica
Costa Blanca
Costa Brava
Costa del Sol
Costa Rica
Crete
Croatia
Denmark
Dubai
Fiji Islands
Florence
Florida
Florida Keys
French Riviera
   (Côte d'Azur)
Gran Canaria
Hawaii
Hong Kong
Hungary
Ibiza
Ireland
Ireland's Southwest

Israel
Istanbul
Jakarta
Jamaica
Kathmandu Bikes
   & Hikes
Kenya
Kraków
Kuala Lumpur
Lisbon
Loire Valley
London
Los Angeles
Macau
Madrid
Malacca
Maldives
Mallorca
Malta
Manila
Melbourne
Mexico City
Miami
Montreal
Morocco
Moscow
Munich

Nepal
New Delhi
New Orleans
New York City
New Zealand
Oslo and Bergen
Paris
Penang
Perth
Phuket
Prague
Provence
Puerto Rico
Quebec
Rhodes
Rome
Sabah
St. Petersburg
San Diego
San Francisco
Sarawak
Sardinia
Scotland
Seville, Cordoba &
   Granada
Seychelles
Sicily

Sikkim
Singapore
Southeast England
Southern Spain
Sri Lanka
Stockholm
Switzerland
Sydney
Tenerife
Thailand
Tibet
Toronto
Tunisia
Turkish Coast
Tuscany
Venice
Vienna
Vietnam
Yogjakarta
Yucatán Peninsula

INDEX